STUDIES IN ECONOMIC AND SOCIAL

This series, specially commissioned by the Economic History Society, provides a guide to the current interpretations of the key themes of economic and social history in which advances have recently been made or in which there has been significant debate.

Originally entitled 'Studies in Economic History', in 1974 the series had its scope extended to include topics in social history, and the new series title, 'Studies in Economic and Social History', signalises this development.

The series gives readers access to the best work done, helps them to draw their own conclusions in major fields of study, and by means of the critical bibliography in each book guides them in the selection of further reading. The aim is to provide a springboard to further work rather than a set of pre-packaged conclusions or short-cuts.

ECONOMIC HISTORY SOCIETY

The Economic History Society, which numbers over 3000 members, publishes the *Economic History Review* four times a year (free to members) and holds an annual conference. Enquiries about membership should be addressed to the Assistant Secretary, Economic History Society, Peterhouse, Cambridge. Full-time students may join at special rates.

STUDIES IN ECONOMIC AND SOCIAL HISTORY

Edited for the Economic History Society by L. A. Clarkson

PUBLISHED

OTHER TITLES ARE IN PREPARATION

British Entrepreneurship in the Nineteenth Century

Prepared for
The Economic History Society by

P. L. PAYNE

Professor of Economic History
in the University of Aberdeen

Second Edition

MACMILLAN
EDUCATION

First published 1988

Published by
MACMILLAN EDUCATION LTD
Houndmills, Basingstoke, Hampshire RG21 2XS
and London
Companies and representatives
throughout the world

Printed in Hong Kong

British Library Cataloguing in Publication Data
Payne, Peter L.
British entrepreneurship in the nineteenth
century.—2nd ed.—(Studies in economic
and social history).
1. Entrepreneur—History   2. Business
enterprises—Great Britain—History
I. Title   II. Economic History Society
III. Series
338'.04'0941   HC255
ISBN 0–333–45735–8

Series Standing Order

If you would like to receive future titles in this series as they are published,
you can make use of our standing order facility. To place a standing order
please contact your bookseller or, in case of difficulty, write to us at the
address below with your name and address and the name of the series.
Please state with which title you wish to begin your standing order. (If you
live outside the UK we may not have the rights for your area, in which case
we will forward your order to the publisher concerned.)

Customer Services Department, Macmillan Distribution Ltd
Houndmills, Basingstoke, Hampshire, RG21 2XS, England.

Contents

Acknowledgements

I wish to thank the Cambridge University Press and Professor Peter Mathias, editor of *The Cambridge Economic History of Europe*, vol. 7, for kindly permitting me to reproduce several passages from my contribution to that volume entitled 'Industrial Entrepreneurship and Management in Britain, *c.* 1760–1970'.

Note on References

References in the text within square brackets refer to the numbered items in the Select Bibliography, followed, where necessary, by the page number, e.g. [155: *129*]. Other references in the text, numbered consecutively, relate to sources, not in the Select Bibliography, itemised in the Notes and References section.

Editor's Preface

When this series was established in 1968 the first editor, the late Professor M. W. Flinn, laid down three guiding principles. The books should be concerned with important fields of economic history; they should be surveys of the current state of scholarship rather than a vehicle for the specialist views of the authors, and above all, they were to be introductions to their subject and not 'a set of pre-packaged conclusions'. These aims were admirably fulfilled by Professor Flinn and by his successor, Professor T. C. Smout, who took over the series in 1977. As it passes to its third editor and approaches its third decade, the principles remain the same.

Nevertheless, times change, even though principles do not. The series was launched when the study of economic history was burgeoning and new findings and fresh interpretations were threatening to overwhelm students – and sometimes their teachers. The series has expanded its scope, particularly in the area of social history – although the distinction between 'economic' and 'social' is sometimes hard to recognise and even more difficult to sustain. It has also extended geographically; its roots remain firmly British, but an increasing number of titles is concerned with the economic and social history of the wider world. However, some of the early titles can no longer claim to be introductions to the current state of scholarship; and the discipline as a whole lacks the heady growth of the 1960s and early 1970s. To overcome the first problem a number of new editions, or entirely new works, have been commissioned – some have already appeared. To deal with the second, the aim remains to publish up-to-date introductions to important areas of debate. If the series can demonstrate to students and their teachers the importance of the discipline of economic and social history and excite its further study, it will continue the task so ably begun by its first two editors.

The Queen's University of Belfast   L. A. CLARKSON
                                                              General Editor

1 Introduction

The quality of British entrepreneurship in the nineteenth century is continually being reassessed. Until the mid 1960s a major *leitmotiv* in accounts of British economic development from the heroic days of the Industrial Revolution to the eve of the First World War was the steady dissipation of a fund of entrepreneurship which, it has been implied, reached its greatest abundance during and immediately after the Napoleonic Wars. From being organisers of change who were 'instrumental in delivering society from the fate predicted for it by Malthus' [254: *129*] by having the 'wit and resource to devise new instruments of production and new methods of administering industry' [172: *161*], British entrepreneurs had, by the latter decades of the nineteenth century, come to be responsible for Britain's failure to retain its role as workshop of the world. Britain's international economic dominance, once so obvious, had been yielded to indefatigable and enterprising American manufacturers and their 'drummers' (commercial travellers), and to persevering, multi-lingual, scientifically-trained Germans.

The fundamental cause of this relative decline, the subject of so much controversy, seemed incontrovertible: there was a weakness in entrepreneurship. The conclusion of Burnham and Hoskins, following a careful study of the iron and steel industry, seemed to have a general applicability: 'If a business deteriorates it is of no use blaming anyone except those at the top, and if an industry declines relatively faster than unfavourable external and uncontrollable factors lead one to expect, the weakness can only be attributable to those who are in control of its activities' [79: *271*]. And these, it was widely believed, had 'grown slack, [had] let . . . business take care of itself, while . . . shooting grouse or yachting in the Mediterranean'.[1] This argument seemed attractively persuasive to many students of economic history. Nobody except examination candidates desperately short of facts, understanding or time, expressed it in quite such simple terms, but even those who entertained grave misgivings about the general condemnation of the British entrepreneur gave it some credence, and those for whom the entrepreneur and his shortcomings represented a major element in any explanation of Britain's loss of industrial leadership were greatly encouraged by David Landes's masterly contribution to the *Cambridge Economic History of Europe* in 1965 [241], perhaps the most eloquent expression of the hypothesis of entrepreneurial failure.

Thereafter a reaction took place. Detailed case-studies and the application of econometric methods resulted in a more sympathetic understanding of the problems of confronting the British entrepreneur. Indeed, in 1971, McCloskey and Sandberg, leading advocates of quantitative assessment, came to the conclusion that 'It is fair to say . . . that the late Victorian entrepreneur . . . is well on his way to redemption' [247: *108*]. Nevertheless, some economic historians continued to entertain doubts about the validity of some of the assumptions underlying the statistical manipulations involved in the quantitative approach, and case-studies sufficiently detailed for quantitative judgements were still all too rare.

In the last few years, much new material has appeared, some of which permits the employment of new methods of analysis, and new criteria for judging entrepreneurial performance have been suggested. Yet there remains much to be discovered about the nineteenth-century entrepreneur and his influence on British economic performance. This brief essay can do little more than attempt to indicate the course of the debate so far and to speculate upon some of the relevant themes. The sheer inconclusiveness of the discussion is challenging, so many questions are as yet unanswered, so much new material – in the form of business archives – is becoming available for research. It may well be that explorations in this most difficult territory will never result in completely satisfying conclusions, but there is no denying the fascination attached to the study of this facet of British economic history.

2 The Entrepreneur: Role and Function

Ideally, one should begin with a universally acceptable definition of the concept of entrepreneurship, but it is a peculiarity of this branch of economic history that it has been plagued with almost as many essays discussing the function of the entrepreneur as with detailed case-studies of his actual role at different periods of time.

Now one and now another prime characteristic has been emphasised. Economists have stressed innovation, risk-bearing, organisation and leadership, sometimes arguing that many other functions performed by entrepreneurs are more strictly managerial; but definition in these terms involves further problems. Exactly what is meant, for example, by innovation? Must it mean doing something that has never been done anywhere before (Schumpeter's concept), or can it mean bringing into an industry something which has been done before but not in that region or in that sphere of economic activity (Fritz Redlich's 'derivative innovation' [212])? This is an important question because, as many of those who have discussed the entrepreneur have to some extent been influenced by Joseph Schumpeter's concept of innovation, there exists a tacit belief that 'entrepreneurship is confined to the big, spectacular, and comparatively infrequent' [234: *112*]. But, as Coleman has observed, 'much activity with an equal right to be called entrepreneurial is carried on in short- or medium-term situations'; and is involved in 'the continuous adaptation of the technical and/or organisational structure of an *existing* business to small changes in the market both for factors and for final products' [*ibid*, emphasis supplied]. Indeed, empirical studies, which reveal the vast majority of entrepreneurs to have been imitative, enhance the correctness of this judgement. They also suggest the abandonment of innovation as a necessary criterion of entrepreneurship and the essential accuracy of G. H. Evans's definition of the entrepreneur as 'the person, or a group of persons, in a firm whose function is to determine *the kind of business* that is to be conducted'. Three core decisions are involved: 'the kinds of goods and services to be offered, the value of these goods and services, and the clientele to be served'. Once these decisions have been made, 'other top-level' decisions have become essentially management decisions – that is, decisions designed to achieve the goals set by the entrepreneurial determination of the kind of business to be operated [184: 25, 252].

Whatever the merits of these, and innumerable other interpretations,[2] few students of economic history would fail to recognise the picture of the entrepreneur provided by Flinn in his provocative essay on the Origins of the Industrial Revolution: '[He] organised production. He it was who brought together the capital (his own or somebody else's) and the labour force, selected the most appropriate site for operations, chose the particular technologies of production to be employed, bargained for raw materials and found outlets for the finished product' [186: 79].

Although Flinn's definition contains elements which Evans might regard as subordinate management functions, any confusion may be resolved if it is understood that the concepts of entrepreneurship and management alter with the changing structure of industry and enterprise. During the Industrial Revolution it is true to say that the entrepreneurs often 'fulfilled in one person the function of capitalist, financier, works manager, merchant and salesman' [254: 132], but a consequence of the slow supercession of the one-man business or the small partnership by the joint-stock limited liability company during the course of the nineteenth century was not only that the entrepreneurial role became more specialised – a whole range of functions appropriate to the days of the 'complete businessman' being shed – but that the association, rather than the individual, came to perform this role [170: 5].

Developments in the capital market – including, for example, the financial activities of the legal fraternity, the evolution of country banking and the rise of the provincial stock exchanges [180] – coupled with changes in company law, permitted entrepreneurs to finance their undertakings with funds other than their own (for a magnificent regional example, see [115]). The function of the capitalist became a separate one. Furthermore, whereas the sheer novelty of many of the inter-related problems exercising the pioneers had, in the absence of technical and commercial expertise within the firm, the locality or even the economy, to be solved personally, with growing experience, and the evolution of specialised intermediaries in many branches of industrial and commercial activity – factory architects, consulting engineers, accountants, selling agents, and the like – the solution to questions that once had necessitated the master's decision were capable of being handled by the managerial staff, or partially determined by specialists employed either within the organisation or as consultants. Hence, in the larger concerns, a second functional split occurred between those who made strategic decisions, the senior partners on the board of directors acting as a team (albeit one sometimes drawn entirely from a single family or from a small group of related families), and those who kept the firm going from day to day, the managers or the administrators.

Thus, as the century progressed, the entrepreneur, acting either as an individual or jointly with others in an organised association, having set up his business or taken over an existing one, could confine his activities to determining major policy decisions involving, *inter alia*, the exploitation of technical and/or organisation innovations and the continuous adaptation of the firm so as most profitably to exploit his chosen markets. The problems associated with the entrepreneurial function may not have been significantly reduced, but the necessity of personally mastering the details of a host of technological and commercial activities certainly had. In the biggest firms, such as the reconstituted Calico Printers' Association, decisions by the executive directors came to be based on the reports of advisory committees [51: 528–9]; smaller firms commissioned reports from consultants; and even newcomers to many branches of economic activity, indistinguishable in many ways from their classic forebears, could usually obtain, for example, accurate performance specifications from those who supplied their machinery and plant, information sadly lacking to the pioneers. In some ways it was all made easier, and in so far as the decision-makers were no longer operating solely with capital provided by themselves, less risky. But was the response to less difficult conditions a growing laxity, a diminution of entrepreneurial energy and application?

This brief discussion is intended not merely to introduce what is to many an interesting problem in semantics, but to draw attention to the implications of the dynamic nature of entrepreneurship, and to indicate the necessity of an excursion into the evolution of the structure of the business firm in nineteenth-century Britain.

3 The Structure of the Firm in the Nineteenth Century

As late as 1919 Marshall – with an unrivalled knowledge of institutional arrangements – could write that until 'not very long ago the representative firm in most industries and trades was a private partnership . . . [45: *314*]. Indeed, throughout most of the nineteenth century, the *fundamental* business unit was the individual proprietorship or partnership [33: *111*; 8: *10*]. This was not *simply* a consequence of the Bubble Act of 1720, whereby the creation of a joint-stock company with transferable shares and corporate status was possible only with the consent of the State, but because there appears to have been no pressing necessity to depart from the traditional organisational framework [26: *27*].

There are several reasons for this. The common law partnership – based as it was on professional and commercial skill and personal knowledge – possessed many advantages as a form of business organisation. To some extent it may legitimately be regarded as the product of risk-avoidance. By the unification of ownership and control, the entrepreneur was able to reduce the real or imagined dangers inherent in trusting his business – or even part of his business – to a manager, when the growing size of his firm or his own increasing infirmities necessitated some delegation of authority. Instead, the more capable and conscientious employee who had risen to a position of some managerial authority within the concern would be offered a partnership, thus ensuring that his own fortunes were intimately bound up with the more wealthy, if not the original, partners [209: *150–1*].

This, moreover, represents but one illustration of the inherent adaptability of the partnership form. What is remarkable about those associations that are well documented is their kaleidoscopic nature. Partnerships were created, supplemented, and frequently terminated when conditions called for change. The principal entrepreneurs associated with others in the same or in related

14

branches of activity, both to enlarge the scale or scope of their original enterprises, and to acquire the co-operation of those who possessed some area of expertise in which they themselves were relatively deficient. Examples of the former motive are legion. Extremely elaborate partnership systems were built up by Richard Arkwright [204: *232*; 284: *78*], David Dale [111: *171–2*], James and Kirkman Finlay [258: *4–30*] and the Peel family [269: *80–4*]; but no less interesting are those partnerships which brought together persons possessing complementary skills and talents. Boulton and Watt [330] and Wedgwood and Bentley [305] are perhaps the best-known cases.

The fact that the common law partnership was sufficiently elastic to accommodate the introduction of new partners possessing either capital or expertise, and was so employed, cannot but shed some doubt on the notion of the entrepreneur as typically the owner-manager, which historians have perhaps too readily taken over from the classical economists. Undoubtedly, many early entrepreneurs did conform to this 'ideal' and did perform the entire range of roles suggested by Wilson [254], but probably more common were small, often family-linked, partnerships, reliant in varying degrees on capital provided by sleeping partners, whose active members concentrated on different entrepreneurial functions. Indeed it would be surprising had this not been so, for there is some evidence that the successful performance of different tasks calls for individuals with different personality traits [173: *107–12*].

But, leaving aside internal questions, what was remarkable was the ability of manufacturing and trading partnerships to grow without recourse to the corporate form of organisation. The practice of self-financing, coupled with a growing reliance on an increasingly sensitive network of monetary intermediaries [115], was able to meet the capital requirements of most firms. The essential simplicity of so many of the productive processes, characterised as they were by a growth pattern involving simply the multiplication of units, rather than by radical reorganisation, *permitted* continued direction by the single entrepreneur, or by the small group of enterprises far bigger than had once been thought feasible. The word 'permitted' has been emphasised because Gatrell has demonstrated the apparent absence of any overwhelming benefits of scale in the very industry, cotton textiles, which might have been expected most fully to have experienced such benefits

15

[18]. But when the capital requirements of some enterprises necessitated a very large partnership, to which the descriptive term 'society' or 'company' was frequently applied, the prohibition on claims to corporate status and on the free transferability of shares became more and more irksome, and those growth-inhibiting technicalities stemming from the Bubble Act, which could not be circumvented by the ingenuities of the legal profession, were increasingly ignored. DuBois's study makes it clear that the unincorporated joint-stock company became of significant importance in the decades preceding the repeal of the Bubble Act in 1825, particularly in insurance, the mineral industries and the brass and copper trades (13: *220ff*; 26: *21ff*].

Whatever success such unincorporated companies enjoyed, and however well legal disabilities were repaired in the opening decades of the nineteenth century, the liability of all partners remained unlimited. The inevitable consequence was that 'no prudent man [could] . . . invest his surplus in any business that he [could not] himself practically superintend' [26: *29*]. The principle of limited liability was finally adopted in 1855 only after heated debate, but it is significant that the initial impetus to change was provided by 'a group of middle class philanthropists, most of whom accepted the title of Christian Socialists', who wished to create 'facilities to safe investments for the savings of the middle and working class' [56: *419–20*], and by London financial interests which sought profitable industrial outlets for potential investors [29: *10*], not by those who argued in terms of freedom of contract or by the industrialists themselves, whose voices were seldom heard in the discussions that preceded the Joint Stock Companies Act of 1856 and 1862 (56: *432*].

The response of the industrialists to this legislation confirms their muted interest.[3] Although by the mid 1870s the limited company had secured a foothold in almost every branch of economic activity, in 1885 such companies account for, at most, between 5 and 10 per cent of the total number of important business organisations, and only in shipping, iron and steel, and cotton could their influence be said to have been considerable [29: *105*; 52: *56ff*]. Although the firms that were limited were by far the most important in their spheres of activity, judged by size of unit and amount of fixed capital, the vast majority of the manufacturing firms of the country continued to be unincorporated family businesses in the mid 1880s

[8, vol. III: *203*; 53: *171–3*]. Nevertheless, by the mid 1860s a legal structure existed in Great Britain which made fundamental changes in the structure of the individual enterprise possible. The way was open for the emergence of the corporate economy, even though few trod the path. In contrast with the expectations, even intentions, of the statesmen responsible for the early Company Acts, there developed the private company (legally unrecognised until 1907) [27]. Since many of the concerns adopting this form of organisation had previously existed as partnerships or joint-stock companies, the object of private registration was to obtain limited liability while retaining the original management and maintaining the privacy of the past. Further growth was made possible, but only to the extent of the capital of the shareholders named in the Articles of Association, and the introduction of new entrepreneurial talent to the board was inhibited [51: *520*; 58: *408*]. Thus entrepreneurs operated within organisations which show little alteration from those of their pioneering forebears. Certainly there was little movement towards the differentiation of management from ownership, towards the elongation of organisational hierarchies.

It would appear that the experience of Thomas Vickers was not untypical. Giving evidence to the 1886 Commission on the Depression in Trade and Industry, he said that 'it has been an advantage to my company to be a Limited Liability Company – because I have always had as much power as a director of this company as I had as a partner and the resources of the company are greater than the resources of the old partnership.' Indeed, the witnesses from the northern industries constantly reiterated that the direction and management of their concerns were usually identical with those of the former partnerships. The adoption of corporate status with limited liability frequently meant that the technical ownership of many businesses, while sometimes in more hands, had not yet changed the groups of leading entrepreneurs [29: *116, 118, 403*]. This was especially so when 'outsider' investors were allowed to purchase only non-voting securities, such as preference shares and debentures [10: *164*; see also W. J. Reader's 'Reflections on the History and Nature of the Limited Liability Company' in 50: *192, 197*].

Alongside these superficially transformed enterprises were 'the vast majority' of manufacturing concerns, which as late as the mid 1880s preferred the old ways, whatever legal provision for growth

17

and change may have been open to them. Clapham has indicated the branches of industry which remained dominated by family businesses in 1886–7:

> all, or nearly all, the wool firms; outside Oldham, nearly all the cotton firms; and the same in linen, silk, jute, lace and hosiery. Most of the smaller, and some of the largest, engineering firms, and nearly all the cutlery and pottery firms, were still private. Brewing was a family affair. So, with certain outstanding exceptions, were the Birmingham trades and the great, perhaps the major, part of the shipbuilding industry. In housebuilding and the associated trades there were very few limited companies; few in the clothing trades; few in the food trades . . . Merchants of all kinds had rarely 'limited' their existing firms, and the flotation of a brand new mercantile company was not easy. Add the many scores of thousands of retail businesses, 'unlimited' almost to a shop. [8, vol. III: *203*]

There is, then, little evidence of any significant divorce of control from ownership before the end of the century. Substantial growth in the size of the average firm – difficult though it is to measure [51: *519*] – appears to have taken place without any appreciable dilution of proprietorial control. This may be explained partly by the nature of the growth pattern, characterised as it frequently was by the multiplication of existing plants and processes producing a fairly limited range of related products, rather than by bold diversification (which might have necessitated the recruitment of executive talent from outside), and partly by the evolution of a network of trade associations, in the absence of which many shaky firms may have been absorbed by their more enterprising competitors into amalgamations of sufficient scale to have made a more bureaucratic internal structure imperative.

But even this latter development was not inevitable. At the close of the nineteenth century there took place a burst of very large mergers in branches of the textile industry and in brewing, iron and steel, cement, wallpaper and tobacco [21; 43; 63], and if there was one common characteristic of the giant businesses which resulted, it was the great extent to which the vendors retained their hold over their businesses when mergers took place [51, section 2]. Thus, even in the relatively efficient and integrated Associated Portland Cement Manufacturers Ltd, there were, in addition to the managing directors, no less than forty ordinary directors who were appointed because 'there were so many individual interests that had to be considered since it was most important to retain the services of all those who had been most instrumental in conducting the business' [43: *114*]. And when the Imperial Tobacco Company was formed in 1901 the attitude of the heads of the original family businesses was, Sir Wilfred Anson said, 'not unlike that of the thirteen States of America, who, when the federal constitution was first adopted by the United States, gave the central government as little authority as possible and retained as much as they could in their own hands' [14: *65–6*].

Similar sentiments were expressed about the Calico Printers' Association, formed in 1899 by the amalgamation of fifty-nine firms controlling about 85 per cent of the British calico-printing industry and having an original capital of £9,200,000. This giant concern was to be described in 1907 as 'a study of disorganisation' [43: *xi*]. In addition to the heavy burden of over-capitalisation, the Association handicapped itself still further by creating a board of directors of eighty-four members, of whom eight were managing directors. In fact, the 'administration resembled the crude democratic expedient of government by mass meeting'. 'The Directors were but imperfectly acquainted with each other or, what was of great importance, with each other's views' [51: *528*]. It remained for the vice-chairman of English Sewing Cotton Ltd – another great concern suffering similar initial difficulties – explicitly to draw the obvious conclusion, applicable to a large proportion of the giant British combines, that 'it was an awful mistake to put into control of the various businesses purchased by the company the men from whom the businesses were purchased, because these men have got into one groove and could not get out of it' [43: *133–4*]. The consequence was unwieldy boards of directors, frequent breakdowns of internal communications, and an unwillingness on the part of the branch managers of the numerous obsolescent units in each combine to accept the closure of inefficient works.

In the majority of cases such difficulties were eventually overcome by schemes involving the reconstruction of the ailing giants and by new methods of management,[4] and inasmuch as an increasing proportion of the larger firms came to be controlled by directors whose total shareholdings represented an ever-diminishing minority of the equity capital, the roots of managerial capitalism can dimly be perceived in Britain before the First World War as well as the eventual domination of the nation's economic structure by the corporate enterprise [23]. What is surprising is the tenacity throughout the nineteenth century – and beyond – of forms of business organisations characterised by a marriage of ownership and control almost as complete as that encountered during the Industrial Revolution [53: *173, 180–1*].

4 The Entrepreneur: Origins and Motivation

In 1948 Ashton showed that the pioneer industrialists 'came from every social class and from all parts of the country' [172: *16*; see also 204: *376–82*]. Although subsequent enquiries [notably 73; 84; 85; 108; 164; 174; 189; 194; 226] have vastly increased our knowledge of this entrepreneurial class and its geographical, social and occupational origins, generalisation regarding the relative contributions of each distinguishable group remains hazardous. Crouzet's estimates are undoubtedly the best and most comprehensive yet devised [181]. By collecting the overwhelming majority of the published data about the origins and careers of the men who pioneered the new industrial system, and by employing in their analysis realistic definitions of such concepts as occupation and social class, he confirms the growing belief that only a relatively small proportion of 'the true industrialists, the founders of relatively large undertakings' [181: *139*] came from the upper class or the lower orders. Recruits from the middle ranks of society, frequently with mercantile connections, appear to have predominated. Crouzet reveals that although many of the early industrialists had humble – though not proletarian – backgrounds, upward social movement did take place on such a scale and in such a way that it *is* possible to speak of the self-made man; that 'rags to riches' is not entirely a myth; that there was intra-class if not inter-class mobility. 'Most people who benefitted . . . rose *within* the middle class, from its lower strata (in some cases on the fringe of the working class) to a new stratum of wealthy, or at least well-to-do industrialists' [181: *142*]. Acknowledging that his carefully constructed sample is unscientific, Crouzet has concentrated upon the major figures 'about whose career[s] *some* information was available'. These were a minority, surrounded, in almost every branch of industry, by swarms of small firms, operated by men who can be assumed to have had more modest origins. They constituted, he aptly suggests, 'a reserve army of capitalists' from whose ranks a substantial propor-

21

tion of successful industrialists arose. Crouzet believes that industry itself 'bred a large number of the leaders who "revolutionized" it', that a powerful process of endogenesis was at work. [181: *116*]

Essentially, these were Katrina Honeyman's conclusions. In each industry she examined, 'there was a paucity of new blood. Leadership was either entrenched because of the traditional nature of the industry [lead mining], or, in the case of the new industries, it was recruited from a less developed branch of the same industry [fustian masters and calico printing moved into spinning; silk merchants and manufacturers into hosiery]' [194: *166*]. For all that, the building up of 'samples' inevitably suffers from serious weaknesses. As Charlotte Erickson was to write of a later generation of industrialists in steel and hosiery, they 'represent the proportion of the whole population which the historical sources enabled us to study' [182: 7]. What of the regiments of the anonymous; of those whom many economic historians have depicted 'as ants tirelessly maximising profits to lift the graph of economic growth'[5] by participating in short-lived partnerships, leaving perhaps only an entry in the docket books in the Court of Bankruptcy [44]?

It is because all the individual 'samples' embodied in Crouzet's study are themselves inherently biased towards the successful that dangers are involved in too ready an acceptance of the apparent correlation between Dissent and entrepreneurial activity. Flinn, who provides the best introduction to this long-debated topic, takes as a basic assumption 'a substantial disparity between the proportion of non-conformists in society and the proportion who were successful entrepreneurs' [187: *25*]; then, building on the work of McClelland [203] and Hagen [189], he seeks to explain this in terms of achievement motivation operating through systems of child upbringing which were themselves significantly influenced by religious persuasion. The argument is convincing, but the suspicion remains that the over-representation of non-conformists among the *entrepreneurs who attained prominence* may be explicable not in terms of their religious precepts, their superior education or their need for achievement, but because they belonged to extended kinship families that gave them access to credit which permitted their firms, and their records, to survive, while others, less well connected, went to the wall.

Be that as it may, the early entrepreneurs, whatever their geographical, occupational or social origins, were similarly motivated. They sought to enrich themselves. Yet as Perkin has observed, 'the limitless pursuit of wealth for its own sake is a rare phenomenon', and he quotes Adam Smith approvingly: '"to what purpose is all the toil and bustle of the world? . . . it is not vanity which urges us on . . . it is not wealth that men desire, but the consideration and good opinion that wait upon riches.". . . The pursuit of wealth was the pursuit of social status, not merely for oneself but for one's family' [208: *83*], and this often meant the acquisition of a landed estate, the purchase or building of a great house, and the quest for political power, either on the national or the local scene. It was always so, before, during and after the Industrial Revolution [234: *95ff*].[6] Only the relative attractiveness of land, the stately home, and the title of nobility or knighthood as symbols of social advancement appear to have varied over time;[7] and those who have argued that this pursuit of non-economic ends inevitably involved a haemorrhage of entrepreneurial talent as the nineteenth century progressed [237: *190–1*], should perhaps balance this against what might be called the demonstration effect of conspicuous consumption or social elevation on the new men crowding in to emulate those who had already succeeded.

One cannot help believing that many new thrusting firms would not have come into existence, or small established companies grown, had not their founders or owners, or their socially ambitious wives, seen or been aware of the tangible results of commercial or industrial success. In one sense there was a need for the 'frenetically tangled French Gothic skylines' of the palaces of the cottontot grandees, the Wagnerian retreat of Sir Titus Salt in the woods above Saltaire, the enormous Old English house built for Sir H. W. Peek,[8] and the metamorphosis of Mr Edward Strutt – who appears to have devoted much of his time to politics and government rather than the direct management of the firm established by his grandfather – into Lord Belper [210: *10–11*]. These manifestations of success served to encourage the others.

Similarly, many sought to establish firms so that the family name might be perpetuated. The attainment of this objective became easier during the nineteenth century. The unincorporated partnership, often embodying in its trading title the names of its more prominent members, was legally terminated with the death of any one of them. If reconstituted, a new collection of names would often replace those of the founders. With the joint-stock form the company could enjoy eternal life. If successful and well respected, commercial considerations dictated the retention of the original name, so that, for example, 'George Green & Co' would continue, albeit with the suffix 'Limited', even if the male members of the Green family – having attended Eton and Oxford – no longer played an active role in the business. They had inherited – and often greatly enlarged – family mansions, picked up a knighthood or even a peerage, perhaps for political services, and seen the fountainhead of their wealth prosper under the guiding hands of the new generation of professional executives, drawn sometimes from a less affluent branch of the family. There was no need to suffer any loss of identity.

Indeed, some economic historians, almost invariably citing the case of Marshall's of Leeds [326], have seen in this waning of the entrepreneurial energies of the founders' descendants a plausible reason for Britain's disappointing economic performance in the late nineteenth century [214: *563–4*; 45: *91–2*]. The seeds of ultimate decline of Rathbone Bros & Co merchants of Liverpool, for example, are clearly visible by the late 1860s when 'money ceased to be much of object [to the partners]' and the firm was 'gradually allowed to run down' so that the members of the family could more actively pursue their own interests in politics, education, philanthropy and religion [308: *120, 128, 131*]. This aspect of business history has been labelled 'the Buddenbrook syndrome' (from the novel by Thomas Mann) and undoubtedly a number of studies furnish some empirical support for it (e.g. [102; 147; 232; 233; 274; 276; 344]).[9] But, as Professor Coleman has observed, if one castigates some second- or third-generation businessmen for quitting their offices and factories one is only blaming them for following a long-established English tradition, and there are, moreover, numerous significant exceptions [278: *270–1*].

Indeed, as yet all too little is known about the age-structure of firms in the nineteenth century. Just how many firms remained under the control of the same family for three generations? And of those that did, what proportion did they consitute of any particular industrial or commercial sector? John Butt found that very few partnerships in the Scottish cotton industry during the industrial revolution were continued for longer than a decade [80: *120*]. 'Of the 135 firms in Leeds engaged in the sale and manufacture of woollens, worsteds and blankets [in 1830] only 21 houses had partners who could provide a direct link with those in 1782' [226: *115*]. In Oldham, it was said that of 138 concerns in existence in the town in 1846, only four had been in possession of the same firm or family before 1800 [89: *23*]; and in 1891 the Rev. M. Anstey of Leicester calculated that in the previous twenty-eight years, of 105 firms that began business in the hosiery trade, 27 had failed, 27 had closed down through making no profit, 13 had transferred their businesses into other hands, no information was available on 21 and only 17 firms were known still to be in business [168: *176*].[10] A comprehensive study of the early Scottish limited companies formed between 1856 and 1895 showed that the *average* length of life of those involved in manufacturing exceeded twenty years only in textiles, clothing and footwear (21.1 years); in chemicals and allied products, the average length of life was but ten years [52: *101*]. Facts such as these lead one to suspect that only a very small proportion of firms created and continued by deed of partnership in the first half of the nineteenth century or incorporated in the latter half of the century survived more than thirty years, a period insufficiently long to sustain more than two generations of a founding family [see 53: *190–2*; 154: *111*]. This is not to imply that the Buddenbrook syndrome does not exist – indeed, some interesting examples can be found [278: *270–1*] – but that its influence in the nineteenth century is of little significance.

When the data collected in the course of creating the *Dictionary of Business Biography* [198] and the *Dictionary of Scottish Business Biography* [219] are fully analysed,[11] they will almost certainly reveal *inter alia* that in the older firms control was increasingly exercised by those brought up to a life-style foreign to the founding fathers, and that during the course of the nineteenth century some degree of formal education became increasingly necessary for business success. But, above all, the relatively narrow base of British industry (cotton textiles, iron and steel, and heavy engineering) coupled with a slowly changing structure, made for the continuation – even strengthening – of the process of endogenesis. Certainly the provisional findings of David Jeremy [199] and Christine Shaw [218] strongly suggest this possibility. The great majority of those 'captured' by the *Dictionary of Business Biography* 'came from relatively prosperous backgrounds; were well educated by the standards of the day' and 'began their careers by working their way . . . in their family business' [218: *38, 16*].

This is in marked contrast to the general spirit of the assertion by Samuel Smiles who, in his famous work *Self-Help* (first published in 1859), observed that

The instances of men . . . who, by dint of persevering application and energy, have raised themselves from the humblest ranks of industry to eminent positions of influence in society, are indeed so numerous that they have long ceased to be regarded as exceptional [221: *47–8*]

If business leaders *were* drawn predominantly from the middle class during the pioneering period, how much more likely is it that the area of recruitment was similarly restricted as the nineteenth century advanced? There undoubtedly occurred a diminution in the opportunities open to those in the lower reaches of the middle class and a positive contraction of those confronting the artisans and the working class, if only because, as free grammar schools were converted into fee-charging schools and boarding schools and free places transformed into scholarships requiring expensive preparation, the chances that the educational system offered to the sons of manual workers became increasingly circumscribed. Upward mobility for the working class by this route was, Perkin has indicated, probably at its nadir in the second half of the nineteenth century [208: *426–7*]. Chapman and Gatrell can detect a constriction of the area of recruitment in the cotton industry from as early as the mid 1820s [89: *20*; 18: *124–5*] and Howe's study [196] reveals that the increasing capital size of enterprises in cotton enhanced the position of hereditary owners. Howe's

review of the origins and recruitment of mid-century textile masters reveals . . . a strongly hereditary nucleus. Approximately 54 per cent had succeeded to partnership in their father's firms or had been the sons of textile masters. [Even] where 'new men' entered, the evidence does not suggest a preponderance of lowly-born self-helpers . . . but the entry of men from relatively prosperous commercial, industrial, and professional backgrounds. [196: *8–21*]

Although it is conceivable that some branches of engineering were not inimical to entry by talented persons of relatively humble origins throughout the century, it is almost certain that more typical was iron and steel which, Charlotte Erickson has shown, became increasingly closed, exclusive and patrician in its recruitment [182: *189, passim*; 208: *426*], and coal, where 'the social composition of the business élite . . . seems to have narrowed during the late nine-teenth century . . . and business leadership became increasingly inbred' [94: *449–68*].

With the notable exception of what are generally known as the 'Oldham limited liability companies',[12] the public company probably suffocated the entrepreneurial aspirations of the lower middle strata of society. Possessing few, if any, shares; names which had no attraction for the potential investor; and at best only the most tenuous connections with other firms, there was no room for them on the board. Their career ceiling in such concerns was in the ranks of management. Even the railway companies, which, as Gourvish has shown [188], did much to raise the status and augment the role of the non-owning, salaried manager, appear to have recruited the majority of their chief executives from those who possessed considerable initial advantages of birth and education. Their origins were predominantly upper-middle and upper class; and it is not, therefore, too surprising to find that a high proportion of them gained seats on the board, for their social backgrounds were similar to those of their erstwhile employers.

Thus, the creeping dominance of the economy by corporate enterprise apparent at the turn of the century, coupled with the necessity of even larger initial capital stocks, even for relatively small-scale manufacturing partnerships, may have made for a situation in which what Chapman and Marquis aptly called 'the movement of work people against gravity' [178: *299*] became increasingly rare.

If much of the foregoing is offered, as Church has observed, 'in the subjunctive mood' [7: *20*], there seems to be general agreement upon Rubinstein's thesis that 'where there was commerce, finance or trade, money was made more readily than where there was manufacturing industry' [213: *619*]. If it is correct to argue that the entrepreneurs in the late eighteenth and nineteenth centuries sought to enrich themselves, then their chances of doing so appear to have been much greater in a London counting house than in a Lancashire factory or a Clydeside shipyard: 'it is clear that the wealthy earned their fortunes disproportionately in commerce, finance and transport – that is, as merchants, bankers, shipowners, merchant bankers and stock and insurance brokers – rather than as manufacturers and industrialists' [213: *605*; 7: *24*]. Although it is almost impossible not to be convinced of the essential accuracy of Rubinstein's argument (which seems likely to be confirmed by the findings of the *Dictionary of Business Biography* [198]), the case of William Todd Lithgow is a salutory reminder of the possible inadequacy of executry records in assessing the wealth of the industrialist [313].

5 The Quality of Entrepreneurial Performance

(i) THE INDUSTRIAL REVOLUTION: A CASE FOR REASSESSMENT?

The poverty of information on so many aspects of the study of British entrepreneurship has not inhibited economic historians from making assessments of the quality of entrepreneurial performance. Attention has mainly been directed to the closing decades of the nineteenth century, but a proper appreciation necessitates a much broader comparative view. To assert, as Aldcroft did in 1964, that '. . . entrepreneurial initiative and drive were flagging, particularly before 1900' rests partially on the assumption that 'the British entrepreneur had lost much of the drive and dynamism possessed by his predecessors of the classical industrial revolution' [227: *114*]. But is this assumption fully justified? And, furthermore, does a consideration of 'drive and enthusiasm' constitute an adequate basis for judgement? Surely, other criteria, such as knowledge and skill, are involved?

Such questions have so far attracted little systematic analysis. Perhaps the very paucity of scholarly business histories has inhibited such inquiries, but it is more likely that, overwhelmed by a belief that an economic transformation *did* take place between, say, 1780 and 1830, there has been too ready an acceptance of the idea that the entrepreneurs, the chief instruments of change, must deserve their reputations for courage and adventurousness, progressive efficiency, organisational ability and grasp of commercial opportunity, combined with a capacity need to exploit it. But do they? This is too large a theme for adequate treatment here, but recent studies raise the suspicion that the eulogistic aura enveloping the pioneers has been somewhat obscuring, if only because it is becoming increasingly clear that earlier assessments of the entrepreneur – which have been implicit rather than explicit – have reflected a biased sample. If nothing else, there is a possibility that the majority of records that have been located and 'worked' for this period – and these, it will be freely admitted, are few in number – are predominantly those of concerns that were sufficiently successful to have created conditions favourable for untypical longevity. Hence the survival of their archives.

On the basis of this biased sample, the temptation has been almost irresistible not merely to reconstruct a composite 'complete businessman', possessing all, or nearly all, the virtues, but to extrapolate these qualities not only to the many hundreds whose concerns have been mentioned in the county histories and the accounts of local clergy, but even to those whose names have *never* been recorded, to those in the ranks of the stage armies of 'early cotton manufacturers' or 'ironmasters' deployed by economic historians. It is possible that such a procedure is misleading. Recent research depicts the Industrial Revolution in a much more negative light than was the case even as recently as a decade or so ago. Crafts's work [11] lends weighty support to Cannadine's observation that the industrial revolution was 'a limited, restricted, piecemeal phonomenon, in which things did *not* happen or where, if they did, they had far less effect than was previously supposed' [4: *162*]. This is not the place to discuss the historiography of the industrial revolution; suffice it to say that if the economic significance of the period *c.* 1760–1830 has been diminished, so too has the status of its traditional heroes. The fundamental changes introduced in certain industries, so comprehensively surveyed by Pollard [209], cannot be denied, but the new interpretation of the 'heroic' period does strengthen the belief expressed in the first edition of this essay that many who succeeded in the early years may not have fared so well in later decades; that, in fact, the ancestors of the much maligned later Victorian businessmen may not have been superior entrepreneurs in every facet of business activity.

It should be remembered that many industrial pioneers operated in what was in some ways a uniquely favourable economic environment. They faced a buoyant domestic market buttressed, particularly in cotton textiles, by a flourishing overseas demand in the exploitation of which they enjoyed monopolistic advantages. So great were the profit potentials at the turn of the century that many entrepreneurs, such as Robert Owen [209: *246*], Benjamin Gott and his partners [115: *240*, *277*] and George Newton and Thomas Chambers [70: *156–61*], who fortuitously caught a rising demand, could often amass sufficient funds to enable their companies to weather later economic storms [180: *162–222*]. The consequence was, as Lee has told us in his study of McConnel and Kennedy, that 'the young man with ability but necessarily endowed with capital could begin business . . . without being doomed to fail' [300: *145*]. Then, following a period of rapid capital accumulation made possible by high initial profits [18: *96, 100*], a policy of 'scrupulous caution' often permitted impressive growth in the size of the firm to take place. And those who have emphasised the risks involved in pioneering – pointing to crises induced by the weather, by the sudden collapse of inherently shaky financial institutions, and by disasters outside the control of the individual manufacturer – should perhaps give greater weight to the widespread existence of fraudulent practices [44: *366*] and to the fact that the severity of entrepreneurial difficulties was often exacerbated by feverish over-production. 'Here as in England business is overdone; the Manchester houses have manufactured enough yarn to serve the world for four or five years', wrote one disappointed partner from Boston in 1809 [270: *286–7*]; an error of judgement so often encountered in the literature that it cannot but diminish any estimate of the commercial acumen of the cotton entrepreneurs, for all the difficulties encountered in obtaining the latest 'market intelligence'. It was the generally favourable demand situation which sometimes allowed the perpetration of the grossest errors to go unpunished by bankruptcy.

Jennifer Tann's investigation of the letters sent to Boulton and Watt clearly reveals that entrepreneurs with exceedingly little technical knowledge were prepared to risk large sums of money in manufacturing ventures and, having done so, to build a factory the size of which was determined not by rational calculation of power supply or transport costs but 'by the capital available for investment on a long-term basis and the maximum output that the entrepreneur thought he could achieve within that limit' [222: *27*; see also 86: *15*]. Not surprisingly, apparently suicidal imbalances of power supply, mill-capacity and potential demand for the product often resulted, and optimal factory layouts were rarely achieved. In Leeds, wrote William Brown in 1821, few flax mills were 'without some defect or other in the height, length, width or shape of the rooms and where irregularity exists in the building complications and confusion must be running in all directions and cards and frames standing in all positions' [222: *33*].

31

Some of these planning imperfections – which could conceivably have led to business failure later in the century – might have been remedied had more of the earlier industrialists developed accurate accounting techniques.[13] These could have served as a guide to costing, but even one of the more talented and efficient entrepreneurs, George Lee – responsible for the building and equipping of the Salford Twist Mill – was forced to admit to James Watt Jr that his production techniques had outrun his knowledge of 'keeping manufacturing Books – in the construction of machinery we never could reduce it to regular piece work or divide the labour of Making and Repairing it in such a manner as to determine the distinct cost of each' [222: 27, 39]. And with a few exceptions, notably Josiah Wedgwood or Boulton and Watt, these plaintive words probably represent the unspoken views of the vast majority of entrepreneurs in all branches of economic activity. Pollard's explanation of the failure to develop to any considerable extent the use of accounts on guiding management decisions is significant: '. . . the problem calling for a solution was not widely or continuously felt . . . . Apart from certain crisis years, anyone with a better technique had no problem in selling, and new techniques were so obviously "better" that it did not need elaborate accounts to prove this' [209: 248], but more plausible are Patricia Hudson's observations on the West Riding woollen manufactures whose 'desire for confidentiality and secrecy of affairs meant that most [of them] preferred to do their own accounting and the sheer burden which this involved militated against the adoption of more tedious profit calculations and double entry methods' [115: 236]. In Wales only the larger firms had appointed 'accountants' by the 1820s [121: 89] and there is some evidence, from the Crawshay ledgers, that 'in many ways there was less detailed [costing] information being disclosed in 1825 than in the early years of the firm's existence' [121: 136].

These remarks are not intended to belittle the achievements of the entrepreneurs of the Industrial Revolution. Their object is twofold: to emphasise the need for more detailed comparative investigations of the responses of entrepreneurs to the difficulties that confronted them in the context of the overall economic environment within which they operated; and to suggest that the names that have become famous (Arkwright, Oldknow, Strutt, Peel, Owen, McConnel and Kennedy, Gott and Marshall in textiles; Crawshay, Lloyd, Reynolds, Roebuck, Walker, Wilkinson, Boulton,

Watt, Bramah, Maudslay in iron and engineering; Minton, Spode, Wedgwood in pottery; Dundonald, Garbett, Keir, Macintosh, Tennant in chemicals; Whitbread, Thrale, Truman in brewing) were not typical entrepreneurs. The majority of them conducted their operations on a scale much greater than their less well-known competitors; many of them owed their successful growth to some degree of monopoly power acquired through patent exploitation, the possession of some unique skill, or the differentiation of their products. Certainly, to generalise upon 'the British entrepreneur' on the basis of this sample is illegitimate, particularly if its purpose is to shed discredit upon their successors. It is not inconceivable that more representative were the Wilsons of Wilsontown Ironworks [282], the Needhams of Litton [307], the Austins of Wotton-under-Edge [131: *172, 183–5*], William Lupton of Leeds [226: *112–15*; 115: *passim*], and John Cartwright of Retford [222: *35*; 80: *107–9, 121*]; all of whose concerns suffered from serious entrepreneurial shortcomings coupled with gross mismanagement.

(ii) THE EARLY VICTORIAN DECADES: THE NEED FOR MORE
    INFORMATION[14]

If there is an inadequate and probably untypical collection of scholarly studies on which to base an assessment of the performance of the industrial pioneers, this aspect of the three or four post-1830 decades is currently even worse served. Neither is the immediate future position very promising. Whereas several collections of business records of the classic period of the Industrial Revolution have been carefully preserved and studied, the overwhelming majority of those of the early Victorian period have either been destroyed or have not yet attracted much attention. Analysis is thus either impossible or insubstantial. Not until the legal requirements associated with the adoption of corporate status guaranteed the retention of certain basic records by *going concerns* is it possible even to begin to assess the role of entrepreneur with any confidence, and even then the surviving sample of archives is unlikely to be representative simply because the records of those firms which were wound up or liquidated have usually disappeared.[15]

This is a grave misfortune. Many of the problems of the pioneers had been surmounted; relatively sophisticated managerial techniques evolved; and the markets of the world, many growing in depth, long remained open to British exploitation – for several decades competition from foreign manufacturers was of little significance. Such was the development of the home and overseas markets, the former enjoying a remarkable buoyancy with the coming of the railway and gradually rising living standards, that the British entrepreneur had no great inducement to alter the basic economic structure painfully evolved in the pioneering period; textiles and iron remained supreme. Not without reason Samuel Smiles was able to write: 'Anybody who devotes himself to making money, body and soul, can scarcely fail to make himself rich. Very little brains will do' [220: *107*].[16]

Even Marshall argued that

> rich old firms could thrive by their mere momentum, even if they lost the springs of energy and initiative. Men whose childhood had been passed in the hard days before the repeal of the Corn Laws; who had come to business early in the morning and stayed late in the afternoon; who had been full of enterprise and resource, were not infrequently succeeded by sons who had been brought up to think life easy, and were content to let the main work of the business be carried out by salaried assistants on the lines laid down in a previous generation. But yet so strongly were such men supported by the general inflation of prices, that in most cases they made good profits and were satisfied with themselves. Thus an extraordinary combination of favourable conditions induced undue self-complacency. [45: *91–2*]

But how far are Marshall's strictures correct, or even fair?

Immediately, the question arises of how many concerns were in fact controlled by the sons or nephews of the founders. The point has already been made that all too little is known about the age-structure of firms in this, or indeed in any other, period of the nineteenth century. With the ever-changing internal power structure of partnerships and the high rates of dissolution and liquidation [48; 52], it is possible that the controlling interest in relatively few firms remained in the hands of the founder's immediate family beyond two generations. We are perhaps too eager to generalise from the records of those that did, forgetting that our inadequate sample is far from random. This is not to say that entrepreneurial weaknesses did not exist – though this is as yet unconfirmed, it is simply to argue that it is potentially dangerous to set too much weight on any proposition that is dependent upon the mere passage of generations.

It has already been noted that the absence of any dramatic change in the scale of operations, the relatively slow enlargement of the labour forces of individual enterprises, and the close coincidence of firm and plant, coupled with the fact that the majority of large companies were but 'private firms converted', meant that the nature of entrepreneurship and the structure of the firm changed but little in the middle decades of the nineteenth century. Influenced no doubt by the relatively high rate of economic growth, burgeoning exports and apparently rapid technological diffusion, there has been little or no retrospective criticism of the early Victorian entrepreneur. Yet the decline of a number of hitherto leading firms can be traced to this period. 'The Final Phase' of Marshall's of Leeds set in during the mid 1840s, though this once great firm was destined to linger on for another forty years, by which time many of its leading competitors in flax spinning had already gone: Benyons in 1861, John Morfitt and John Wilkinson a few years later and others, including W. B. Holdsworth, soon following [326: *199, 229*].

The Ashworth cotton enterprises, built up between 1818 and 1834 by Henry and Edward Ashworth – 'among the most renowned of the men who followed the great inventors and . . . took the cotton industry forward by "assiduity, perseverence, attention to detail, minor improvement"' – began their relative decline in the 1840s, when the partners' will to expand withered away before diversifying interests, growing internal tensions, and low profits and even losses. In 1846 George Binns Ashworth, Henry's son, noted that:

> in the new Eagley Weaving Shed there were no costings, no control of quality, no regular stock-takings; customers suffered from late delivery, and often the lengths of cloths were shorter than had been ordered. Owing to technical and managerial defects the looms now ran for hardly half the working day and total production was much below that of their competitors.

Although this was perhaps the worst of the firm's periodic managerial lapses, after 1847 things improved, but the firm never regained its earlier technical pre-eminence: 'Fortunes now will only be made by intense plodding and keenness', noted George Binns Ashworth in his diary [263: *14, 42, 31*].

One who failed to 'plod' was James Thompson of the Primrose Works, near Clitheroe. Perhaps the leading firm in the calico-printing trade, his exclusive prints – in the design of which he called upon 'the talent even of Royal Academicians' – were specifically manufactured 'for the upper hundreds, and not for the millions'. Heedless of warnings by the young Lyon Playfair, who became chemical manager of the works in 1841, that the business was doomed unless he changed the character of his product, Thompson refused to abandon his short runs. 'His products were known all over Europe for their high excellence, and he could not bear to lower . . . their quality.' 'It was a common saying of Thompson that "once you become a Calico printer there are but two courses before you – the *Gazette* or the grave".' In the event, he died a disappointed man, in 1859, but a few months before his famous works were closed [324: *43–4, 52–6; 78–81*]. Other calico printers had, however, attempted to produce for the million instead of the few and to do so had cut their costs to the bone by the debasement of design and by trying to convert 'herds of Lancashire boors into drawers, cutters, printers, machine workers, etc.' at appallingly low wages. Not surprisingly the products were execrable and failures numerous. As John Dugdale, owner of the Lowerhouse Print Works, near Burnley, observed in 1847: 'If yo'll look back for th' last six years, yo'll find half o' th' Printers are brocken – an' half o' those that are left canno' break, for nobody'll trust 'em, and the rest get on as weel as they con' [165: *73*].

Courtaulds got on very well. When Samuel III went into semi-retirement in the mid 1860s, the partners (now George Courtauld III, Harry Taylor and John Warren) enjoyed enormous incomes – the fruits of the efforts of an earlier generation – while allowing the firm to fall technically far behind other silk throwsters and manufacturers. Indeed, George Courtauld III 'contributed virtually nothing but inertia to the family business'. Only a buoyant and inelastic demand for its main product, ritual mourning crepe, coupled with falling raw silk prices, permitted the enterprise to make its handsome returns on capital at a time when its senior partner brought to the family firm none of 'those qualities of vigour, perception, intelligence, and enterprise' to which it owed its establishment by his uncle [278 vol. I; *174–7, 213*].

In iron, Joshua Walker & Co. did not long survive the end of the Napoleonic Wars, its steel trade being formally wound up in 1829, and the iron trade finally wasting away by the early 1830s [296: *29–31*]. Other ironmasters fared little better. John Darwin, sometime associate of Peter Stubs and one of the leading Sheffield industrialists, had gone bankrupt by 1828 [260: *41–2*; 75: *161–2*]; many vanished in the middle decades of the nineteenth century, among them Lloyd, Foster & Co., of Wednesbury, the first exploiters of host-blast and, later, the Bessemer process in the Black County [75: *156*]. Even the Coalbrookdale Company, bereft of managerial guidance when Abraham and Alfred Darby retired (in 1849) and Francis Darby died (in 1850), faltered, sustained only by sheer momentum and a continuing demand for the products of its foundry [320: *270*]. In South Wales, William Crawshay II, regarding his family as 'Iron Kings and Cyfarthfa as the crown they wore, wanted to dictate terms and force his own ideas upon the buyers'. The Guests of Dowlais 'might send agents to Russia to canvas for orders but Crawshay sat in his counting house and orders came [or failed to come] to him' [256: *120–6*].

Though these examples could be multiplied nothing can be proved by them. They are mentioned merely to indicate the desirability of additional research into the quality of entrepreneurship in the staple British industries during the decades following the heroic age of the Industrial Revolution, and to suggest the possibility that many more firms would have gone down in this period had they been confronted by the degree of competition encountered by their successors; that, in fact, 'a decline in entrepreneurship' can be selectively exemplified at almost every time and in almost every well-established branch of trade. Certainly the closing decades of the century possess no monopoly of this phenomenon.

Nevertheless, in one respect there *may* have been a difference between the pre-1870 and post-1870 decades. Towards the end of the latter period, whatever ingenious defences the 'new' economic historians have engineered to re-establish our faith in the quality of British entrepreneurship in cotton, coal, and iron and steel, there is no gainsaying the belated recognition of the growth and profit-potential of motor cars, some branches of chemicals, electrical engineering and the like. Few such significant failures to appreciate the *new* can be perceived in earlier years.

Take the possibilities for entrepreneurial resource engendered by the boundless demand associated with the coming of the railways. The number of patents taken out relating to railway equipment in the middle decades of the century was enormous. Everywhere, the engineers of the railway companies and freelance inventors developed their own devices to provide greater efficiency, safety and comfort, and the manufacture of many of their gadgets was taken up both by railway companies and by outside firms, some of which were literally brought into being to exploit railway patents. George Spencer & Co., for example, was created to work Spencer's own conical rubber buffer, draw and bearing spring patents of 1852 and 1853 and those granted to P. R. Hodge, J. E. Coleman and Richard Eaton. Similarly, John Brown of Sheffield, quickly perceiving the need for more powerful buffers as locomotive rolling stock outgrew plain wooden headstocks or horse-hair pads confined by metal bands, was already building his fortune on the manufacture of steel helical or volute buffer springs and, as early as 1855, was said to dispense no less than £5000 annually in 'getting people to uphold' his product, a sales technique which, coupled with a willingness to provide long credits and even take payments in shares, made him Spencer's most formidable rival in the ensuing decades [318: *2–3, 73–4*].

Other firms owed their origins to success in the desperate scramble to gain sole licences to work the patents of the host of railway inventors. Forges and brass- and iron-foundries came into being or were expanded in order to make innumerable fittings for locomotives and carriages, signals and lights, which, since they were specified for use in the construction of a particular locomotive or carriage design, the railway company workshop, locomotive builders or carriage and wagon manufacturers had no option but to 'buy in' [318: *138–41*]. Indeed, the engine and rolling stock works, spawned by the dozen in the middle decades of the century by the railway companies themselves and by outside initiatives, were the pioneers in the process whereby complicated machines and vehicles came to be assembled from a wide range of component parts of metal, wood, leather, glass, textile and rubber, for the most part manufactured by a host of suppliers working to exact specifications and, in the case of moving parts, to very close tolerances [103].

There was, in this instance, apparently no hesitation in taking up new things, adopting new production techniques, devising new modes of organisation, and fashioning new and flexible marketing organisations and techniques. Is this rapid appreciation of the new perhaps the *only* significant difference between the middle years of the nineteenth century and the two or three decades preceding the First World War? Or is this too an illusion, a consequence of the non-existence of competitive economies elsewhere against which to measure the mid-Victorian achievement? Indeed, how does one measure entrepreneurial capacity? 'The answer', as Saul has argued, 'may lie in a series of international comparisons' [248: *394*], but what if this technique is, as in the present case, inappropriate? Can one then employ the concept of export market shares? Hardly, in a period when Britain was virtually in a monopolistic position, enjoying the benefits of an early start. It might be possible to analyse deviations from what is apparently best practice in particular industries, though here one runs the real danger of equating 'best' with 'most recent'. It is enough to say that at this juncture there is insufficient information to assess mid-Victorian entrepreneurship in any meaningful sense.

Some firms which traced their origins to the Industrial Revolution were declining in relative importance; some were disappearing altogether; others were crowding in to take their chances in both old and new fields of enterprise. There were many who shared with Josiah Mason, the steel-pen maker and pioneer of electro-plating, a 'quickness in seizing a new idea . . . sagacity in realising the possibilities of development, and . . . courage in bringing it within the range of practical application' [257, vol. I: *151*], though few shared his great success. Yet an economic historian is ill-equipped to judge the technical feasibility of the thousands of inventions whose specifications – often deliberately obscure in their wording – line the walls of the Patent Office. How can one estimate what profitable opportunities went unexploited? It is not enough to say what had been done; it is necessary to assess what might have been done and was not. Not until the Americans, the Germans and the Belgians were in a position to undertake a range of manufacturing activities comparable with that of the British can innovatory negligence even begin to be appraised, though one would guess that in the middle decades of the nineteenth century such cases were few in number.[17]

But to point to the enthusiasm for taking up patents as an indication of energetic and adventurous entrepreneurial behaviour may be partially misleading, for it is equally capable of illustrating the adoption of tactics designed to permit survival rather than innovation and growth. The refusal of so many family concerns even to contemplate the adoption of the joint-stock organisation

39

condemned the majority of them to remain limited in size. Given that many branches of economic activity experienced growing competition in the middle decades of the century, an increasing number of firms attempted to differentiate their products, frequently by concentrating on lines at the top end of the price range that exhibited craftsmanship and individual character. Alternatively, or even additionally, they could specialise in the manufacture of goods 'protected' – however dubiously – by a patent. Immediately the product was endowed with an inalienable uniqueness.

Almost equally powerful a weapon of sales strategy was the adoption of a distinctive trade mark of 'brand'. There was nothing new in this technique – once again it was well known to Wedgwood – but it seems to have been increasingly adopted in the middle decades of the century.[18] It must have received a considerable boost from the Great Exhibition of 1851, as a result of which the names of many firms and their products first became known nationally, even internationally. By advertising the medals won, by announcements in newspapers, by posters on railway stations, and above all by the 'pushing' of commercial travellers and commission agents, the product could sometimes attain a reputation for superiority over the basically similar offerings of competitors. (For case-studies, see [318: *95–113*; 122: *251*; 262: *29–331*; 339].)

By increasing specialisation designed to exploit marginal differences in quality or design, and by creating the impression that the differences were greater than they were in reality, many British firms were able to secure a degree of oligopoly power. This attempt to insulate themselves from the pricing policies of their rivals was in several instances sufficiently successful to permit some concerns to reap relatively high profits on a relatively small capital and turnover, even if this involved the exploitation of regional rather than national or international markets.

The policy of product differentiation, however, may well have had the consequence of depressing the national rate of economic growth. Many small firms were able to make comfortable profits, and were strengthened in their resolve not to increase the scale of their operation beyond the size which would have involved partially entrusting their businesses to managers recruited from outside the family circle. But having consciously decided to restrain the growth of the firm within the limits of existing managerial resources, such concerns were often ill-equipped to exploit overseas markets, even when it was considered desirable or necessary to do so.

At home a number of travelling salesmen might be employed to 'cover' the intended market and, since their remuneration was usually partly dependent upon the volume of sales, there was every likelihood that they would 'push' the firm's product vigorously. However, a permanent sales force of this kind was apt to be expensive, particularly in the early days of a firm's existence, and it was often supplemented by a network of strategically located commission agents. Selling through agents was particularly attractive to the relatively small concerns anxious to minimise direct selling costs and desirous of stabilising marketing expenses as a percentage of sales, particularly when the market for the product was characterised by seasonal or cyclical fluctuations. Furthermore, commission agents often enjoyed greater accessibility to certain trades because of previous or current experience with a related line.

Nevertheless, this mode of marketing possessed inherent disadvantages in the British context. So many British firms were small that agents would rarely act solely for one manufacturer. This often inhibited the continuous promotion of specific products; the agent varying his effort in accordance with the relative salability of the lines he represented in order to maximise his own income rather than the sales of the products of any one of his clients. Indeed, there is a possibility that a commission agent will deliberately refrain from maximising sales volume for fear that he will be replaced by a salesman when a certain level of business has been obtained. The inherent weaknesses involved in the use of commission agents were greater in overseas than in domestic trade where, because of distance, language difficulties and unfamiliarity with the market, the manufacturer had even less control over the agent sales force than at home. Partial representation was more likely since overseas agents tended to act for a greater number of firms, and the direct contact between the manufacturer and buyer was often so attenuated that inadequate market intelligence sometimes led to defective or apparently lethargic entrepreneurial response.[19]

In many cases, of course, there was no direct contact between manufacturer and consumer. Many manufacturers were wholly or partly dependent on wholesaling factors and merchants for the distribution of their goods.[20] This was the case, for example, in hardware, tinplate and many kinds of textiles. Furthermore, it is clear that many intermediaries required that their trademarks be put on goods manufactured by their suppliers, whose manoeuvrability and marketing strength must thereby have been greatly weakened, if not completely surrendered. Not the least important consequence of the manufacturers' dependence on 'the wholesale people' was the multiplicity of shapes, sizes and designs that they were expected to produce, for it was in the interests of the wholesale merchants to be able to offer a comprehensive 'range'. This method of marketing also made possible the continued existence of numerous small, often weakly-financed family concerns, many of whom chose to specialise in the exploitation of but a limited portion of the full spectrum of demand for related products.[21]

It would appear that the majority of British firms – whether their products were sold directly to the consumer or through intermediaries – became increasingly specialised during the middle decades of the nineteenth century. It was an ideal way to get started and, having become established, to survive. But as the author has argued elsewhere:

specialisation, for whatever cause, tends to become increasingly irreversible, for there takes place a concomitant growth of special mercantile relationships, highly skilled labour forces and the evolution of particular types of managerial talent that makes any return to an earlier, more flexible, position more expensive and difficult. Thus, all too many British entrepreneurs ceased even to consider the possibilities of diversification, of branching out into entirely new lines of production where more profitable opportunities may have existed. Faced with an apparently limited market for the existing range of products, failure to grow was often incorrectly attributed to demand conditions rather than to the limited nature of entrepreneurial resources. The firm's resources, both material and entrepreneurial, had, in fact, become characterised by a high degree of "specificity". In many cases this inevitably involved a limitation of the firm's horizon of expectations and this constituted a barrier to further growth. (51: *525*]

It is apparent from the records of many of the West Riding wool textile firms [115: *251–2, 311*, note 50] and from the private ledgers of several Scottish firms that investment expenditures shifted from activities within the firm to investment in the equity of unrelated outside companies (for an interesting example, see [128: *13–15*]).

Growth did not constitute a major desideratum of the majority of British firms; they wished to remain small enough to permit supervision and control by the family. And if their profits were considered adequate – and product differentiation often meant relatively higher profits per unit of output – can they be criticised for so doing? It is unrealistic to suppose that entrepreneurs should be completely immune from experiencing an increasing desire to substitute leisure or political power, or prestige from philanthropic works, for income maximisation after a certain conventionally acceptable income level had been attained or a fortune acquired.[22] The danger involved is not only that the national rate of economic growth will fall below its potential or even optimum level – since, as Hobsbawm has emphasised, there is no necessary correspondence between the interest of the individual firm and the economy [25: 187–91] – but that any future acceleration will be jeopardised.

It is arguable that in the mid nineteenth century British industrial organisation, characterised by the family firm, became partly ossified at a relatively immature level of development, and that this structure remained largely undisturbed even when the legal obstacles to the growth of firms were removed in the mid 1850s. The consequence would have been less severe had it not been for the fact that to combat foreign competition successfully in the closing decades of the century demanded large units enjoying lower unit costs, and marketing arrangements more sensitive than those that were an inevitable corollary to the small-scale firm.

(iii) 1870–1914: THE CRITICAL PERIOD?

One of the most stimulating debates by economic historians in the last two decades concerned the competence of entrepreneurs in late-Victorian and Edwardian Britain. Exercised by the need both to understand and to explain the declining rate of growth of industrial production, the relative deterioration in the international position and the sluggish rise in productivity, there has been an almost overwhelming temptation to adopt – in varying degrees – the suggestion of many critics that 'to an indefinable but considerable extent leadership was not wrested from Britain, but fell from her ineffectual grasp' [140: 230]. Even those who have vigorously denied this proposition have reluctantly conceded that there might be something in it. 'It may be', wrote Saul, in an earlier study in this series, 'that after all is said and done, the entrepreneur and his shortcomings remain to provide the residual explanation for Britain's weaknesses' [55: *51*].

In summarising the case for the prosecution, Landes, acknowledging an element of caricature, found that British enterprise reflected a:

> combination of amateurism and complacency. Her merchants, who had once seized the markets of the world, took them for granted; the consular reports are full of the incompetence of British exporters, their refusal to suit their goods to the taste and pockets of the client, their unwillingness to try new products in new areas, their insistence that everyone in the world ought to read in English and count in pounds, shillings, and pence. Similarly, the British manufacturer was notorious for his indifference to style, his conservatism in the face of new techniques, his reluctance to abandon the individuality of tradition for the conformity implicit in mass production. [241: *564*]

Aldcroft, in his first tentative exploration of the role of the British entrepreneur, reached the 'inescapable' conclusion that 'the British economy could have been made more viable had there been a concerted effort on the part of British enterprise to *adapt itself more readily*' [227: 134]; and Levine, after examining a number of possible explanations of industrial retardation, concluded that 'technical and organisational lag in British industry was, more than anything else, a question of entrepreneurial responses' [243: *150*].

In this brief essay it is impossible to do justice to these authors. Their works all repay close study; and Landes's sophisticated reasoning is especially compelling. Indeed, his contribution to the *Cambridge Economic History of Europe* (subsequently reprinted with minor revisions and chronologically extended to the present day as *The Unbound Prometheus*) represents the high-water mark of the critical school. Although Habakkuk's remarkable essay, *American and British Technology in the Nineteenth Century* [237] – which drew attention to the possibility that British entrepreneurial shortcomings could be explained as a consequence of a slow rate of market growth, and that lack of adventurousness and dynamism in many branches of British industry was a logical response to demand

44

conditions – provoked Landes into a brilliant rearguard action in 1965 [242], the hypothesis of entrepreneurial failure took 'quite a beating' in the late 1960s [246: *393*].

The attack on this hypothesis took several forms. It was pointed out that the student was being asked to accept a quantitative conclusion – that the detrimental effect of entrepreneurial deficiencies on the performance of the British economy was highly significant – on the basis of a qualitative argument; one moreover that rested on a somewhat narrow basis of fact. McCloskey and Sandberg emphasised Landes's heavy dependence on illustrations drawn from Burn's and from Burnham and Hoskins's studies of the British steel industry, and, less fairly, on 'a few . . . cases in chemicals, electrical engineering and a handful of other industries' [247: *97*]; and Sigsworth noted that Aldcroft's assertion that 'studies of the individual business firms confirm the belief that entrepreneurial initiative and drive was flagging, particularly before 1900' rests upon four such case-histories [252: *21*].

Characteristically, the response of British economic historians was to re-examine and broaden the factual base. Thus, Charles Wilson enlarged the scope of the enquiry by drawing attention to the entrepreneurial activities of those beyond the 'frontiers of pig iron and cotton stockings' to those engaged in the 'new industries, where the factory was encroaching on old craft, and the multiple on . . . the village shop', to the manufacturers of soap, patent medicines, mass-produced foodstuffs and confectionery; to the great publishers – George Newnes and Alfred Harmsworth – and to a miscellaneous collection of international freebooters who were carving out commercial empires abroad [255: *194–5*]. Although Saul's comment on this argument 'by example' was that it was hardly convincing [55: *62*], he was guilty of adopting a similar approach, albeit one with much greater analytical depth and penetration. His armour-piercing bullets – compared with Wilson's buckshot – were, appropriately, directed at the machine tool and mechanical engineering industries, which he found displayed many praiseworthy features. He made it plain that their very real commercial and technological successes had been generally underestimated [152; 153; 154; 229; and see the discussion by Floud, 107].

Meanwhile, the authors marshalled by Aldcroft [229] to examine a number of major British industries in an endeavour to refine his own earlier critical evaluation of the British entrepreneur were beavering away among the reports of government Commissions and Select Committees, trade journals, business histories and all manner of secondary sources to discover (perhaps to the editor's, perhaps to their own, surprise?) that really hard evidence of entrepreneurial failure was remarkably elusive. Indeed, Sigsworth, faced with this survey of British manufacturing industry, asked:

> can we still continue to generalise with such certainty about the characteristics of "the British entrepreneur" between 1870 and 1914? It is not simply that as *between* industries, British entrepreneurial performance was "patchy" and that a patchiness existed in "old" industries as well as "new", but that *within* industries (e.g. engineering, iron and steel, glass, wool textiles), there existed marked differences in performance between different sections and, within sections, between different firms. And if the diversity of experience appears even stronger than has hitherto been conceded, can we continue to accept generalised explanations about characteristics which, in so far as they amounted to 'shortcomings" or even "failure", were so variously distributed? [252: *129*]

And the relevance of these questions was enhanced by studies of the British boot and shoe [91], leather [93], and cycle industries [112].

But the British approach of piling case upon case, despite the increasing sophistication of the analyses, was unsatisfactory to those American scholars who were convinced that the measures of performance employed by Landes, Aldcroft and his associates, Wilson, Church and Harrison, were inadequate on theoretical grounds: 'measures of output because they confound influences of demand with those of supply and the measures of indicative innovations because they neglect the variability in the advantage to be gained from different innovations in different countries' [246: *100–1*]. Essentially, their argument was that the only legitimate way to arrive at a quantitative conclusion concerning the relative importance of entrepreneurial failure – if such proved to exist – was by quantitative methods, the selection of which should be determined by the application of explicit economic models.

As McCloskey and Sandberg, two of the leading proponents of this approach, argued in a very useful paper [247], since assertions of British entrepreneurial failure imply a comparison with superior performance elsewhere, usually in Germany or America, the first desideratum is some yardstick to measure the distance between British and foreign performance. That chosen was the profit forgone by choosing British over foreign methods. In other words:

> The adoption of foreign methods . . . is viewed as a potential investment, and entrepreneurial failure as a failure to make such investments as were profitable. The existence of profitable but unexploited investments is used to gauge whether British entrepreneurs could have done better, and the size of the foregone earnings to gauge the significance for economic growth of their failures to do so. [247: *102*][23]

Perhaps the most rigorous application of the new methodology to British experience was McCloskey's study of the iron and steel industry [129], an industry which had to a special degree encouraged generalisation concerning the economy as a whole. McCloskey argued that the slow adoption of the basic steel-making process (which has been called 'the most notable single instance of entrepreneurial failure') is explicable in terms of technological developments, and that the much-criticised neglect of phosphoric Lincolnshire ores was a rational response in a competitive market to the location of the ores. He was convinced that the British iron and steel masters exploited the potentialities of world technology before the First World War as well as, if not better than, their much lauded American competitors. 'Late Victorian entrepreneurs in iron and steel did not fail. By any cogent measure of performance in fact, they did very well indeed' [129: *127*]. And, in a much slighter and less convincing examination of the British coal industry, McCloskey found that 'the case for a failure of masters and men in British coal mining before 1913 . . . is vulnerable to a most damaging criticism; there was clearly no failure of [labour] productivity' [248: *295*].

Lars Sandberg also returned to the nineteenth-century staples, examining Britain's lag in adopting ring-spinning. Although this has usually been taken as a sign of technological conservatism, not to say backwardness, after a careful analysis of the differences that existed in the benefits to be derived from replacing mules with rings in the United States and the benefits to be derived from doing so in Great Britain, Sandberg concluded that under the conditions then prevailing with regard to factor costs, as well as the technical capabilities of the ring spindles then being built, the British may well have been acting rationally [150: 46]. Furthermore, the same author found no evidence that firms installing automatic looms at the time the cotton textile industry was beginning to be criticised for ignoring them, in the first decades of the twentieth century, expanded faster or made larger profits than their more conservative competitors [150: 82–4].

Indeed, of all the revisions employing econometric methods, only Lindert and Trace – using a cost-benefit calculation to measure the private profits forgone by a non-optional choice of techniques in the chemical industry – discovered an unambiguous case of entrepreneurial deficiency: among those alkali producers who clung to the Leblanc process long after the superiority of the ammonia process, patented by Solvay, was apparent [246: 239–74; for the industrial context, see Warren, 167].

On the basis of these and other studies, McCloskey expressed the belief that there was 'little left of the dismal picture of British failure painted by historians' [247: 459]. But doubts remained. Nicholas questioned the very basis of the methodology employed by the neo-classical cliometricians to show that no productivity failure occurred [250]. Locke criticised their failure to analyse sufficiently the factors involved in calculating cost, profit and productivity [244; 245] and, after reviewing the course of the debate, Crouzet remarked in 1982 that although McCloskey and Sandberg 'thought that they had saved the Victorian entrepreneur from damnation and assured his reputation. . . . Perhaps the wisest solution lies somewhere halfway – leaving many late Victorian entrepreneurs in some sort of Purgatory, undamned but still unredeemed' [12: 412].

So much depended upon what yardsticks were used for the measurement of success or failure: international productivity comparisons? the rapidity of technological diffusion? profitability? the dispersion among various industries of the rate of return to capital? So much of the argument turned upon a consideration of aggregative measures. The firm, which in the nineteenth century was, after all, the engine of economic progress, and the individual entrepreneur tended to get lost. Only Floud applied economic methods (regression analysis) to assess performance at the level of the individual British enterprise – Greenwood & Batley, a leading firm of machine tool makers – and even in this case, with fairly complete statistical data, the findings were somewhat inconclusive if only because it was impossible to determine the precise significance of the growth rate in labour productivity (2.3 per cent per annum) which this firm achieved in the latter part of the century [246: *313–37*].

Nevertheless, one feels that the key to an understanding of the role of the entrepreneur and hence a proper assessment of his performance must be in the analysis of the business records that are now, after decades of neglect, increasingly being located and properly calendared and preserved [349–368]. As Richardson observed, 'what makes a progressive entrepreneur is how he acts in a *given set of conditions*' [229: *276*], and to discover these conditions, which are often highly specific and extremely complex, it is imperative to analyse the letter books, the bundles and files of incoming correspondence, the account books and the internal memoranda of individual firms, and compare the results with those derived from the records of similar firms in the same line of business operating in the same markets.

Only a decade or so ago such a course of action seemed almost utopian; now it becomes increasingly plausible. That formidable difficulties are involved is undeniable, but the effort should be made if only because entrepreneurial behaviour can only be assessed within the context of the individual firm, and an assessment so derived inevitably gains in significance with comparative enquiries into competing firms.[24] There has been all too much criticism based upon social and/or general criteria. To draw once again upon Richardson's pertinent discussion:

> If innovations do not yield reductions in average unit costs, then it would be irrational for a businessman to introduce them even if the innovations would benefit the future growth of the economy. The individual businessman cannot be expected to estimate external economies. The net social returns from investment in innovations may be higher than the private returns, with the result that a capitalistic environment may produce a rate of innovation well below the social optimum [229: *275*];

an argument echoed in Hobsbawm's widely read study *Industry and Empire* [25: *187*].

But the procedure of investigating in detail the surviving records of individual enterprises cannot answer all the questions. One serious deficiency is that it cannot fully reveal why some potentially profitable avenues of enterprise – in, say, some branches of chemicals and pharmaceuticals, electric engineering, domestic equipment, and the like – were either apparently neglected or ignored,[25] simply because inactivity, by definition, can leave no written testimony. In his stimulating survey of *Economic Growth in France and Britain 1851–1950*, Kindleberger has argued that 'social values' must be given the greatest weight in explanations of why new enterprises failed to elbow their way to the forefront in Britain after 1880.

> As business became more complex, the amateur ideal of British society became less sought through accumulation and more through the liberal professions, the civil services, and politics. The attention of people in business drew back from income maximisation. Those outside either found themselves satisfied with social acceptance in a class structure which emphasised cosiness or sought to achieve the upper-middle-class ideal in other ways. The hungry outsiders – immigrants, Quakers, Jews, and lower-class aspirants to wealth – diminished either in numbers or in the intensity of their drive. [32: *133*]

And Coleman's elegant series of variations on the earlier part of this theme, 'Gentlemen and Players' [234], is both thought-provoking and convincing.

There seems little question that many known cases of neglect have correctly been ascribed to the fact that 'the Englishman . . . [had] yet to learn that an extended and systematic education up to and including the methods of original research [was] now a necessary preliminary to the fullest development of industry' [217: *17*]. Landes has pointed to the:

> library of lament and protest about the failure of British educational institutions to turn out applied scientists in numbers and of a quality comparable to those produced in Germany; the failure of British enterprise to use such scientific personnel as were available; the scorn of the body of entrepreneurs for innovations in this domain; and the misuse of such scientists as were employed. [242: *28*][26]

And Coleman [234], Levine [243], Locke [202] and Sanderson [217] have, in their different ways, gone far to explaining these failures, the significance of which seems undeniable, if unmeasurable. Nevertheless, the student of economic history does well to heed Hobsbawm's warning of the dangers of being seduced by 'simple sociological explanations' [25: 189]. Kindleberger implies a diminution in the supply of potential entrepreneurs, but there is no evidence of any such shortage, rather the reverse. It is possible that there were too many entrepreneurs in late-nineteenth-century Britain.

It is not without significance that much of the criticism of the quality of British entrepreneurship is based upon the consular reports, which constitute a veritable 'compendium of derogatory information on British trade' [240, II:26].[27] Even allowing for the fact that 'the consuls reporting were less interested in the aggregate of British exports, or even the total of exports to their own areas, than in the fortunes of specific commodities, the outcome of given contract negotiations, the success of a particular businessman or syndicate' – that, in fact, their accounts 'tended to emphasise the unfavourable news' – there is a verisimilitude about some of the complaints that it would be foolish to deny. One thing is certain: there was 'no phase of the question of foreign competition with British trade abroad on which so much unanimity appears to prevail on the part of Her Majesty's representatives as that of the scarcity of the British commercial traveller'.[28] Why was this? Why was a marketing system so successfully employed in the home market apparently so woefully under-utilised abroad?[29]

The explanation is not simply to be found in the Englishman's traditional abysmal ignorance of, or inability to learn foreign languages. It is more deep-rooted than that. It is related to the structure of British industry itself. The representative British firm was too small to be able to afford a vigorous selling effort in world markets by means of a salaried force of commercial travellers.[30] Hence the continued dependence upon commission agencies and large-scale merchant importers, who, as has been explained, were by no means as 'pushing' as the American and German salesmen employed by much larger manufacturing enterprises.[31] There is no need to labour this point. It is mentioned again simply because it emphasises the necessity – if foreign competition abroad was to be more successfully combated – of an increase in the scale of the average unit in many branches of British industry.

This was not be be: firstly, because of the limitation on growth inherent within the closely controlled private company; and secondly, because many firms were able to avoid losing their identities through amalgamation by means of membership of a trade association. From the viewpoint of enlarged scale this was a double loss. The amalgamation movement was inhibited and the size of the median firm remained small. Furthermore, the industry as a whole 'carried' a number of manifestly inefficient firms. As one witness to the Committee on Trusts explained, although 'it was a law of progess that the inefficient should go . . . in practice progress was impeded because he would not go, so instead of trying to kill him' off, he was pensioned off, 'since that cost far less'.[32]

This policy might have had less detrimental effect on economic growth and less debilitating effects on the export trade if any of the numerous associations which the committee on Trusts revealed had come into being at the close of the nineteenth century had adopted some form of central selling agency, but none of them had. There was 'no counterpart in Great Britain of the German Kartell'[33] whose diligent representatives so impressed the consular officials. Thus the British economy was characterised by relatively small firms whose ability to compete abroad – when, indeed, they made any attempt to do so – was inherently weak,[34] a weakness which was exacerbated by the widespread policy of product differentiation, the successful implementation of which demands continuous personal representation in the market. At home, or in limited regional areas, this could be done; overseas, it was impossibly expensive for the small firm, and of the 'giant companies' that came into existence at the close of the century, few could equal J. & P. Coats, under the redoubtable German salesman, O. E. Phillipi [219: *389–92*], in the efficiency of their marketing organisations.

Instead, resort was made to meeting the most perverse specifications in order to satisfy the customer's often unreasonable demands. British steelmakers offered a multiplicity of shapes and sections [229: *80–1*]; the locomotive and carriage and wagon builders went to almost ridiculous lengths to satisfy the whims of consulting engineers [318; see also 82: *192*]; rarely did a shipbuilder send two similar vessels down the slipways of the Clyde or the Tyne; while at the level of the firm, C. & J. Clark of Street offered literally hundreds of types of boots, shoes and slippers [338: *96–7*]; the number of varieties of biscuits produced by Huntley and Palmers exceeded 400 by the end of the century, many of them specifically for the export trade to which the firm was giving absolute priority [279: *159*]; the early pattern books of the United Turkey Red Company of Alexandria, founded in 1898, contain examples of thousands of prints designed to appeal to the varied tastes of customers throughout the world [362: *52*]; 'Greenwood & Batley made, in the period from 1856 to 1900, 793 differently named machine tools, of which 457 were ordered only once during the period' [246: *321*].

Clearly, in these cases, there was vigour, a responsiveness to the vagaries of demand and the requests of the customers. What is less certain is how representative these examples are. One suspects that the records of the smaller concerns in most industries would reveal a disproportionate concentration on the home market, not because of any lack of trade to be obtained overseas, but because of an intrinsic weakness in the small firm's ability to exploit it. It may be that during the nineteenth century exporting vigour and overseas selling was in direct relationship to the size of the firm, and that the size of the average British firm in most industrial categories was relatively small. If Britain lost her pre-eminence in international trade during the latter part of the nineteenth century more quickly than she need have done (in itself an almost endlessly debatable proportion), this was doubtless partly due not to any general decline in entrepreneurial ability but to a surfeit of individual entrepreneurs, a multitude of aggressively independent firms, each pursuing their own self-interest where any increase in the rate of economic growth demanded more co-operation.[35] But that, as Hobsbawm might put it, could not be expected of an unplanned capitalistic economy.

Only if, as Allen and Lazonick – basing their arguments on brilliant analyses of the North-east Coast pig iron [68][36] and the British cotton industry [123–7] – have argued we abandon the concept of the entrepreneur as a neo-classical manager optimising his profits subject to given constraints, and embrace a Schumpeterian definition of the entrepreneur as one who fundamentally changes these constraints – by, for example, accelerating the speed with which he adopted improved technology (Allen) or by altering the organisational structure that determines technological choices and profitable opportunities, and hence transforming his industrial environment (Lazonick) – can British industrialists be condemned.

Lazonick accuses them of entrepreneurial failure because they failed 'to confront institutional constraints innovatively' [15: 2]. To Lazonick only the replacement of the atomistic, competitive organisation of British industry by a corporate, concentrated, managerial structure capable of superseding the market as an allocative mechanism could British decline be halted or even reversed.

In focusing attention on the question of institutional adaptation, Lazonick and Elbaum have, in effect, given substance to the generalities of Mancur Olsen[37], and doubtless much future work will necessarily be involved with illustrating, refining and assessing their approach, which represents a major advance in understanding Britain's relative decline. It is less clear whether it will further knowledge of the role of the entrepreneur in this decline since it is dependent upon the acceptance of a definition of entrepreneurship which is at variance with that upon which the debate has hitherto been conducted (see the interesting discussion by Harvey [192]).

Recent explorations make it unrealistic to condemn the great majority of British businessmen for the way they behaved *within the context of their individual firms*. Even Lazonick agrees that they 'performed admirably as neo-classical managers – they took the conditions facing them as given and tried to do the best they could' [125:*236*]. It is difficult to accept his corollary that to merit the use of the appellation 'entrepreneur', they *should* have transformed their industrial environment. That they did not do so is not to be explained by reference to 'cultural conservatism', as Wiener has so elegantly argued [253].[38] The questions that need to be answered are: 'How could they?'[39] and equally, if not more important, 'Why should they?', when the problems confronting those who tried were, as Elbaum indicates in his study of the early steel industry [15: *51– 81*][40] all but insuperable; the cost – in profits foregone and the horrendous physical and mental strain involved – so high; and the rewards so uncertain.

Furthermore, would Lazonick's restructuring of the British economy *before the First World War* have retarded Britain's economic decline? It is impossible to say, but the question does suggest a more recent analogy. With the recent and continuing mania for mergers in Great Britain, there is no doubt that institutional rigidities are being eroded. Will British industry be revitalised by the massive restructuring currently underway? It remains to be seen, but it requires the exercise of considerable optimism to believe that the present increase in industrial concentration will necessarily lead to the regeneration of the British economy.

Be that as it may, it is undeniable – as Allen implies [68] – that the rate of British economic growth in the decades before the First World War would have been enhanced had *more* businessmen developed new technologies or new industries possessing high potential levels of productivity. The reason why the British economy failed to generate this desirable response was not so much the fault of the entrepreneur but stemmed largely from the British educational system. Certainly, this was the belief of Herbert Gray and Samuel Turner writing in 1916 [236], and echoed most recently by Correlli Barnett [3] and, even more specifically, by R. R. Locke, whose study demonstrates that the relative decline of the British economy since 1880 can be explained by our inferior and inappropriate educational system [202]. By emphasising the needs of technologically-based industries (and it was here that the British lagged so grievously) and the nature of the new professional skills and business organisations that the growth of the large-scale firm demanded, Locke shows that higher education in Germany – and to a lesser extent in the United States – met these requirements far more successfully than did the British and French systems. It is, moreover, arguable that Britain's education system – and here we are focusing particularly on the primary and secondary level – was also socially more divisive than elsewhere, and that it therefore contributed to the continuance of attitudes and social relations between managers and workers hostile to the development of an efficient, modern economy.

It is not implausible that at a critical time an important sector of the British labour force was, paradoxically, too well-trained (as opposed to being too well-educated), too disciplined and skilled to encourage their employers to abandon handicraft techniques, which in any case were consistent with the tactics of product differentiation. The long-run economic significance of skilled labour, initially postulated by C. K. Harley [238], has received powerful support from W. Lewchuk who, in his studies of the British motor vehicle industry, had emphasised the importance of the associated tradition of labour independence on the shop floor which made it necessary for management to exercise only partial control over labour effort and to depend upon the motivation provided by piece-rates to secure a relatively high and acceptable profit despite low productivity, the malign consequences of which were not fully exposed until the 1960s [15: *135–61*]. It was, moreover, the skill of the British labour force, combined with their appreciation of the 'rules of the game', that inhibited innovation – as Donald Coleman and Christine MacLeod have revealed [235], and as Lazonick has demonstrated in the case of cotton [124] – and so contributed to the relatively low level of investment in Great Britain which, perhaps as much as any other factor, retarded British economic growth.

Additional reasons for the low level of investment in manufacturing activity were undoubtedly the relative attractiveness of the service sector which, it is plain, did not fail to recruit new entrepreneurs [255] and the fact – demonstrated by Rubinstein [213–216] – that money could be made so much more easily in finance than in industry, a point vividly exemplified by Davenport-Hines' masterly study of *Dudley Docker* [280] and by numerous entries in the *Dictionary of Business Biography* [198]. Clive Lee's work [35–38] makes it clear that the expansion of the service sector *during the late-Victorian period* possessed highly beneficial consequences for economic growth and that this growth was neither directly nor in spatial terms immediately dependent upon manufacturing. Thus, the movement into services, to which Charles Wilson drew attention in 1965 [255], provides positive evidence of entrepreneurial perspicacity and vigour in the closing decades of the nineteenth century, and this verdict has recently been strengthened by a number of specific illustrations, among the more notable of which have been those provided by William Rubinstein [198, Vol. 11: *248–64*], Edwin Green and Michael Moss [286], T. R. Nevett [137], Asa Briggs [264], J. W. Reader [322], Clive Trebilcock [341] and Charles Wilson himself [347].

In the context of this exploration of entrepreneurship and British relative economic decline, this movement into services is of the utmost importance. If the 'British entrepreneur' is to be criticised for failing constructively to confront the organisational constraints that were progressively strangling him in the staple industries (industries which were so labour-intensive that Clive Lee has described them collectively as the apogee of proto-industrialisation, rather than the products of an Industrial Revolution), and if he is to be criticised for failing more vigorously to enter new manufacturing industries, then surely this same 'British entrepreneur' deserves some praise for moving into the service sector, whose relatively rapid rate of output growth and high productivity, certainly between *c.* 1870–1913, was so much superior to the old staples that its expansion provided what little buoyancy there was in Britain's aggregate economic growth.[41]

Were, then, the four decades preceding the First World War a critical period of entrepreneurship? The answer must be 'no'. It was simply that with the development of competitive economies, British entrepreneurial errors and hesitation, *always present*, even in the period of the classic Industrial Revolution, became more apparent, and the belabouring of the businessmen who seemed inadequate in their responses mollified the frustrations of those who believed that British industrial supremacy before the mid 1870s was somehow normal and her accelerating relative decline thereafter, abnormal. Rather was it that the whole complex of circumstances that produced British pre-eminence before 1873 was fortuitous. To see the course of British economic development in the nineteenth century in terms of the dissipation of an initial fund of entrepreneurialship is untenable.

6 Conclusions

The one certain conclusion that can be drawn from this all too brief survey is that there is much more to be discovered about the British entrepreneur in the nineteenth century. Charles Wilson's observation remains valid: 'let us not be in too much of a hurry to reach for the black cap: there is more evidence to come'.[42] It is still dangerous to speak of *'the British entrepreneur'*. No such person exists. Over the century there were countless different entrepreneurs in a remarkable variety of trades and industries. Some, perhaps the majority at any one time, were first-generation entrepreneurs, striving to establish a manufacturing firm, a merchant house, a shipping line, and doubtless – if recent enquiries into the small firm are any guide[43] – imbued with enthusiasm and adventuousness; others were the descendants of the founders, apparently less 'pushing', more concerned with order, stability and the sheer mechanics of organisation, to whom the firm was less all-consuming of energy and time; and, during the closing decades of the century, there was a growing number of managers, perhaps from a different socio-economic background, operating within a different institutional framework, and apparently increasingly concerned with the attainment of different objectives.

Indeed, it may be that one element in the lethargic response of some British entrepreneurs to foreign competition in the decades before the First World War was that at the very period when such competition became significant, Britain's industrial structure was being transformed, and that in this transitional stage, during which the dominance of the private company was giving way to the large-scale joint-stock company with limited liability, there was insufficient expertise available to manage the emergent 'giant' enterprises that possessed the potential capacity to grapple with American, German and Belgian competitors (see, for example, the penetrating studies by Locke, [202; 244; 245]). What little is known about the internal organisations of the burgeoning large-scale firms – especially those created by amalgamation and merger – inspires scant confidence in their ability to formulate a swift or appropriate response to conditions of difficulty [52: 534–5].

But when one attempts to understand the specific problems that were being encountered by industrial firms – and this often involves a degree of technical insight with which historians are rarely generously endowed – one can seldom fault the solution arrived at in the light of the available information at the disposal of the entrepreneur or the board at the time of the decision. As Platt has justly observed: 'As historians, we would be unwise to assume that we can judge business decisions by a kind of macro-economic hindsight, by broad economic trends, by developments which may be clear enough to us now but which at the time covered more than a man's working lifetime' [142: 309]. Yet the consequence of envisaging businessmen as neo-classical managers optimising profits subject to given constraints is that it has not been difficult to give them 'a clean bill of health' [190: 121], despite Britain's relatively slow rate of economic growth between the 1880s and the inter-war years and the deterioration of her international position. Should then the application of the term 'entrepreneur' be forbidden to all who failed to lead in the internal transformation of their chosen industries? It seems pedantic to do so, especially when the empirical evidence correlating increased industrial concentration and corporate capitalism to economic growth is so ambivalent.[44]

The current state of the debate on British entrepreneurs before 1914 appears to indicate that as a whole they did not fail, although in certain industrial sectors there appears to have been a failure of entrepreneurship. Such an epigrammatic conclusion is far from satisfactory but it does reveal the desirability of, and scope for further inquiry. The analysis of the data by the editors of the *Dictionary of Business Biography* and the *Dictionary of Scottish Business Biography* [198: 219] should go some way towards extending Charlotte Erickson's work [182] on the social, educational and religious backgrounds of entrepreneurs and top management; but there is still a need to discover more about the motivations of entrepreneurs and the changes in their motivation over time [179]; the longevity of firms in different industries; the influence of institutional arrangements upon entrepreneurial goals; the relationship between size of firm and marketing policies; the possibility, suggested by Checkland, that firms 'cannot adjust to change continuously, but must reach some critical level of vulnerability before a response is forthcoming'.[45] These are but a handful of the themes whose exploration would be enhanced by more evidence. Such comparative investigations are inherently complex, and the less ambitious or less experienced student should remember the continuing need for detailed narratives in a wide variety of business endeavour; analytical case-studies, particularly for the middle decades of the century; and the provision of data permitting inter-firm productivity and profitability comparisons. The range of questions is almost endless; the raw material for research is assuming awesome proportions; new and more precise methods of inquiry are being evolved. One day it may be less hazardous to generalise about different categories of British entrepreneurs. Currently, it is still as dangerous a pursuit as it was a dozen years ago when the first edition of this essay was published, but perhaps therein lies its continuing fascination.

Notes and References

1. Arthur Shadwell, *Industrial Efficiency*, new edn (1909) p. 653. That Shadwell's criticisms were not without foundation is apparent in several recent studies; see, for example, Mary Rose on Edward Hyde Greg [333: *92–5*] Richard Wilson on Sir Walter Greene [198, vol. II: *673*], and Maurice Kirby on Joseph Whitwell Pease [299: *55*].

2. For an interesting discussion of entrepreneurship, business performance and industrial development, see Alford [231]; Casson's economic theory of the entrepreneur [177] is valuable.

3. My own researches into the files of the early Scottish companies [52] makes me very sceptical of Kennedy's argument that '*at the root of this very hesitant development* lay the fact that the legal requirements governing managerial behaviour and the disclosure of company affairs under limited liability were so minimally drawn as to place the company's directors in virtually unchallengeable and unchecked possession of the company's assets' [31: *113*, emphasis supplied].

4. Although, as Lazonick [34: *119–39*] has recently emphasised, this took a remarkably long time.

5. The phrase used by Richard Wilson [226: *122*] which, he asserts, bears no resemblance to the activities of the Leeds merchants.

6. There are, of course, exceptions. For an interesting – if not necessarily typical – example, see Minchinton's study of the tinplate makers of West Wales [134: *106–7*].

7. It has to be said that the motives which inspired some industrialists to invest in land were not confined to the quest for prestige. Mary Rose has shown that the Gregs purchased land because it was safe investment, and 'far from being a hindrance to the millowner, land might prove a positive advantage, by making mortgages easier to obtain in time of need, or by improving the return on capital' [332: *79–88*]; and Hudson has emphasised the importance of the ownership of landed property in gaining access to credit [115: *269*].

8. Details of some of the houses built for Victorian entrepreneurs

61

are provided by Mark Girouard's fascinating study, *The Victorian Country House* (Oxford, 1971); for examples cited, see pp. 7, 8, 184, 186–7.

9. Byres has shown how the Bairds of Gartsherrie conformed to the Buddenbrook dynamic. Control of their great firm passed out of the hands of the family after the impressive efforts of the second generation had given it a position of supremacy in the Scottish iron industry [232, vol. II: *802–6*]. One particularly odious member of the third generation, 'Squire Baird' as he was nicknamed, a backer of prizefighters, had the dubious, if appropriate, distinction of being accorded a pen-picture by the scurrilous Frank Harris in *My Life and Loves* (1964), vol. 3, ch. XIII.

10. It was observed by G. d'Eichthal in 1828 that: 'Throughout Lancashire no family survives longer than two generations. Children brought up to habits of luxury and idleness are incapable of salvaging their business when fortune turns against them' (quoted by Gatrell [18: *117*]). Data on the West of England cloth industry in the first half of the century show a very high mortality rate, and even the names of the relatively few surviving firms may have concealed a change of partners [131: *104–5*]. The volatility of firms in the cotton industry in the early nineteenth century, 'with high exit rates compensated by high entry rates', is demonstrated by Lloyd-Jones and Le Roux [41: *147*].

11. In both cases it is intended to subject the data collected by the galaxy of authors to computer-assisted analysis.

12. For these unique companies, see Roland Smith [160], R. E. Tyson [342; 343], W. A. Thomas [162: *145–68*] and, particularly, D. A. Farnie [104: *244–73*].

13. That some attempted to do so is evident from the pioneering study by Haydn Jones of *Accounting, Costing and Cost Estimation [in] Welsh Industry: 1700–1830* [121].

14. After the first edition of this study appeared, Roy Church subjected this section to protracted critical examination [7: *19–43*]. Since several of his strictures and suggested modifications are not only tangential but rest on foundations 'only marginally less flimsy' than my own, I have retained my original treatment of this period in the hope that it may continue to stimulate constructive debate and inspire further empirical inquiry. I would add only that my own explorations since the early 1970s, primarily into Scottish business archives [141; 52], have proved to be consistent with the majority of

the hypotheses put forward in the following pages.

15. Of the *surviving* 1200 companies of the 30,000 firms registered as companies in London between 1856 and 1889, the majority are concerned with banking, insurance, food, drink and leisure or are professional associations. Industrial concerns are relatively rare. See Richmond and Stockford [365].

16. Professor Church regards this opinion 'as quite simply untenable' [7: *38*] and chastises me for citing it. It must be confessed that I found it irrisistible! This is not the place to pursue our differing interpretations of the period, suffice it to say that the differences between us on the question of profits are briefly discussed by Mokyr [249: *866–9*].

17. It must be confessed that this observation is founded on an acquaintance with a fairly limited range of railway equipment, the technical understanding of which took all too long to acquire.

18. Considerable evidence on this practice is contained in the Minutes of Evidence of the *Select Committee on Trade Marks*, 1862 (212, xii, pp. 431–627). See also Redford [146: *42*], Alexander [65: *114–15, 126, 149*, Jefferys [117: *passim*].

19. For a brief but cogent discussion of the advantages and disadvantages of employing commission agents both at home and overseas, see Stephen Nicholas, 'Agency Contracts, Institutional Modes, and the Transition to Foreign Direct Investment by British Manufacturing Multinationals before 1939', *Journal of Economic History*, XLIII (1983), 677–9.

20. As Platt argues, for the small manufacturer this often made good sense. '"Never thou put salt water between thee and thy money" was the advice which the British manufacturer received from his cradle' [142: *142*].

21. The foregoing argument – based upon a reading of a variety of business archives supplemented by numerous hints in secondary sources – is set down as an hypothesis requiring more rigorous empirical testing. Needless to say, it is only our general ignorance of marketing – and the significance attached to it by the author – which makes its inclusion permissible in a study such as this.

22. As William Rathbone of Liverpool wrote to his wife in July 1869: 'My feeling with a merchant was that when he got over £200,000 he was too rich for the Kingdom of Heaven' [308: *3*].

23. It might be helpful to emphasise a point made by McCloskey and Sandberg:

The opportunities foregone in neglecting the best technique have been expressed in a variety of ways and this gives a misleading impression of heterogeneity of purpose in the new work. The various measures used are essentially identical. Higher profits can be achieved if more output can be produced with the same inputs, that is if productivity can be raised. The measuring rod for entrepreneurial failure, then, can be expressed indifferently as the money amount of profit foregone, as the proportion by which foreign exceeded British productivity, as the distance between foreign and British production functions, or as the difference in cost between foreign and British techniques. All of these give the same result and each can be translated exactly into any one of the others. [247; 103]

For a criticism of the methodological technique involved, see Nicholas [250].

24. It is the consistent appraisal of entrepreneurial efficiency, using a variety of techniques, that makes the studies of shipping companies by Hyde and his colleagues at the University of Liverpool so valuable [293; 294; 308; 309].

25. A formidable list of new inventions and innovations more quickly taken up by Americans and Europeans than by the British was compiled in 1916 by H. G. Gray (a member of the Mosely Educational Commission to the United States in 1903) and Samuel Turner [236].

26. Byatt has illustrated the fact that in the electrical industries, 'British businessmen were not very good at using their engineers' [82: *190*], and Pollard and Robertson that in shipbuilding, 'few builders maintained even rudimentary laboratory facilities or employed *any* scientists' [144: *137*, emphasis supplied].

27. The study by Ross J. S. Hoffman [239] is heavily reliant on this source. It is interesting to compare his findings with those of Platt [142: *136–72*], whose analysis of the same material is much more understanding of economic realities. See also Alfred Marshall [45: *135–6*] and, for a more favourable view of the British overseas marketing performance in the decades before 1914, Nicholas [251].

28. *Opinions of H.M. Diplomatic and Consular Officers on British Trade Methods*, Cd.9078 (1898) p. 5. See the discussion by Aldcroft [230: *295–9*].

29. For comparative figures of travellers in the Swiss market at the

close of the century, see Chapman [6; 253].

30. Some idea of the expenses incurred in overseas representation is given by Platt [142: *143–4*]. See also Payne [318: *190*], Davis [281: *33–5*] and Hoffman [239: *87*]. J. H. Fenner & Co's principal foreign representative, operating in southern and south-eastern Europe, was so generously remunerated with salary and commission that in 1910–13 he was earning more than the company's managing director [281: *33*].

31. For an interesting example – the way in which Singers built up its European markets – see R. B. Davis, '"Peacefully Working to Conquer the World": The Singer Manufacturing Company in Foreign Markets, 1854–1889', *Business History Review*, XLIII (1969) especially 306–11.

32. Ministry of Reconstruction, *Report of the Committee on Trusts*, Cd.9236 (1918), p. 3.

33. *Ibid.*, p. 22. See *Report of the Departmental Committee appointed by the Board of Trade to consider the position of the Textile Trades after the War*, Cd.9070 (1918), p. 113.

34. This argument, based upon business archives to which the author has had access, receives some support from the Bolton Report, *Report of the Committee of Inquiry on Small Firms*, Cmnd.4811 (1971) pp. 37–9.

35. This point was made in a number of reports of the committees set up to consider the position of several trades after the war of 1914–18. See, for example, *Report of the Departmental Committee appointed by the Board of Trade to consider the position of the Shipping and Shipbuilding Industry after the War* Cd.9092 (1918), p. 31, paras. 89–90: 'Whilst individualism has been of inestimable advantage in the past, there is reason to fear that individualism by itself may fail to meet the competition of the future in Shipbuilding and Marine Engineering, as it has failed in other industries. We are convinced that the future of the nation depends to a large extent upon increased co-operation in its great industries.' How the existence of many mutually suspicious firms could constitute a formidable barrier to improvement in an industry is perhaps best illustrated in tinplate [134: *87–8, 198*].

36. Although the central thrust of Allan's article [68] is both sound and stimulating, it can and has been criticised in detail. I am grateful to Dr Gordon Boyce for allowing me to read his unpublished manuscript entitled 'The Development of the Cargo Fleet Iron Co.,

1900–1914: A Study of Entrepreneurship, Planning, and Production Costs in the Northeast Coast Basic Steel Industry'.

37. Mancur Olson, *The Rise and Decline of Nations: Economic Growth, Stagflation, and Social Rigidities* (New Haven, Conn., 1982), see especially pp. 77–87.

38. See the criticisms of Wiener's thesis by Saul [55: *69–70*]; Coleman and MacLeod [235: *599–600*]; McKendrick [42: *101, 103*]; and J. M. Winter [42: 185–6].

39. This is not the place to take up this major question but it is worthy of note that Kennedy [22: *151–83*; 30; 31] implies that even entrepreneurs of Schumpeterian stature would have found it difficult to achieve rapid structural change in the late Victorian economy because of the inadequacies of the capital market, cf. the cogent, if brief, discussion by Lee [37: *66–70*].

40. It is not without significance that Elbaum, Lazonick's co-editor of *The Decline of the British Economy*, remarks in the course of his illuminating paper: 'That British firms none the less lagged behind their competitors was less the result of entrepreneurial failure – *as the term is conventionally understood* – than of the constraints on individual entrepreneurial action posed by market conditions and a rigid institutional environment' [15: *54*, emphasis supplied].

41. Manufacturing labour productivity in the United Kingdom in 1870 was only 71 per cent of that in services; in 1913, only 46 per cent [38, Table 1]. Even so, an important component of the service industries, insurance, has not escaped criticism from Trebilcock for entrepreneurial failings in the late Victorian period [42: *137–72*].

42. C. Wilson, 'Canon Demant's Economic History', *Cambridge Journal*, VI (1953–4), p. 286.

43. See Jonathan Boswell, *The Rise and Decline of Small Firms*, (1973), pp. 36, 68–74; Donald A. Hay and Derek J. Morris, *Unquoted Companies* (1984).

44. See, for example, K. Cowling, P. Stoneman *et al.*, *Mergers and Economic Performance* (1980).

45. S. G. Checkland, review of Coleman's *Courtauld's* in *Economic History Review*, 2nd ser. XXIII (1970), 559–60.

Select Bibliography

Such has been the flood of books and articles on different aspects of entrepreneurship in the past decade that it is impossible fully to recommend a general bibliography to both the subject and the period covered in this essay. That compiled by David Landes for the *Cambridge Economic History of Europe, Vol. VI: The Industrial Revolution and After*, ed. H. J. Habakkuk and M. Postan (Cambridge, 1965) remains valuable; A. E. Musson's list in *The Growth of British Industry* (1978) is useful, as are the 'Notes' to Crouzet's *The First Industrialists* (Cambridge, 1985) and the footnotes to Coleman and MacLeod [197a].

The purpose of this brief bibliography is to provide references to the secondary works upon which this essay is based; to furnish a guide to further reading; and to indicate a number of basic sources which might profitably be consulted by those students seeking to pursue research into those business archives which may, in time, serve to confirm or to deny some of the arguments advanced by those who have rushed to judge the British entrepreneur. The bibliography is roughly divided into six main sections which are not mutually exclusive. The second of these, 'Studies of Particular Industries, Trade and Regions', is particularly selective, the works cited being those which have special relevance to this exploratory essay.

The place of publication is London unless otherwise stated.

I GENERAL WORKS AND THOSE CONCERNED WITH INDUSTRIAL STRUCTURE AND ORGANISATION

[1] T. S. Ashton, 'The Growth of Textile Businesses in the Oldham District, 1884–1924', *Journal of the Royal Statistical Society*, LXXXIX (1926).
[2] W. Ashworth, 'Changes in the Industrial Structure, 1870–1914', *Yorkshire Bulletin of Economic and Social Research*, XVII (1965).

[3] Correlli Barnett, *The Audit of War* (1986).

[4] David Cannadine, 'The Present and the Past in the English Industrial Revolution, 1880–1980', *Past and Present*, No. 103 (1984).

[5] A. D. Chandler, 'The Growth of the Transnational Industrial Firm in the United States and the United Kingdom: A Comparative Analysis', *Economic History Review*, 2nd Ser., XXXIII (1980).

[6] S. J. Chapman, *Work and Wages, Pt I: Foreign Competition* (1904).

[7] Roy Church (ed.), *The Dynamics of Victorian Business* (1980).

[8] J. H. Clapham, *An Economic History of Modern Britain*, 3 vols (Cambridge, 1926–38).

[9] P. Lesley Cook, *Effects of Mergers: Six Studies* (1958).

[10] P. L. Cottrell, *Industrial Finance, 1830–1914. The Finance and Organisation of English Manufacturing Industry* (1980).

[11] N. F. R. Crafts, *British Economic Growth during the Industrial Revolution* (1985).

[12] Francois Crouzet, *The Victorian Economy* (1982).

[13] A. B. Dubois, *The English Business Company After the Bubble Act, 1720–1800* (New York, 1938).

[14] R. S. Edwards and H. Townsend, *Business Enterprise. Its Growth and Organisation* (1958).

[15] Bernard Elbaum and William Lazonick (eds), *The Decline of the British Economy* (Oxford, 1986).

[16] P. Fitzgerald, *Industrial Combination in England* (1927).

[17] P. S. Florence, *Ownership, Control and Success of Large Companies* (1961).

[18] V. A. C. Gatrell, 'Labour, Power and the Size of Firms in Lancashire Cotton in the Second Quarter of the Nineteenth Century', *Economic History Review*, 2nd Ser., XXX (1977).

[19] H. J. Habakkuk, *Industrial Organisation since the Industrial Revolution. The Fifteenth Fawley Foundation Lecture* (Southampton, 1968).

[20] Tom Haddon, *Company Law and Capitalism* (1972).

[21] Leslie Hannah, 'Mergers in British Manufacturing Industry, 1880–1918', *Oxford Economic Press*, New Ser., XXVI (1974).

[22] Leslie Hannah (ed.), *Management Strategy and Business Development. An Historical and Comparative Study* (1976).

[23] Leslie Hannah, *The Rise of the Corporate Economy* 2nd edn (1983).

[24] A. E. Harrison, 'Joint-stock Company Flotation in the Cycle, Motor-vehicle and Related Industries, 1882–1914', *Business History*, XXIII (1981).

[25] E. J. Hobsbawm, *Industry and Empire* (1969).

[26] B. C. Hunt, *The Development of the Business Corporation in Britain 1800–1967* (Cambridge, Mass., 1936).

[27] P. Ireland, 'The Rise of the Limited Liability Company', *International Journal of the Sociology of Law*, XII (1984).

[28] J. B. Jeffreys, 'The Denomination and Character of Shares, 1855–1885', *Economic History Review*, XVI (1946).

[29] J. B. Jeffreys, *Trends in Business Organisation in Great Britain Since 1856* (New York, 1977).

[30] William P. Kennedy, 'Economic Growth and Structural Change in the United Kingdom, 1870–1914' and see the appended 'Discussion' by Ben Baack and Donald McCloskey. *Journal of Economic History*, XLII (1982).

[31] William P. Kennedy, 'Notes on Economic Efficiency in Historical Perspective: The Case of Britain, 1870–1914', *Research in Economic History*, vol. 9 (1984).

[32] C. P. Kindleberger, *Economic Growth in France and Britain, 1851–1950* (Cambridge, Mass., 1964).

[33] D. S. Landes, 'The Structure of Enterprise in the Nineteenth Century. The Cases of Britain and Germany', Comité International des Sciences Historiques, XL Congrès Internationale des Sciences Historiques, Stockholm, *Rapports V: Histoire Contemporaire*, Uppsala, 1960.

[34] William Lazonick, 'Strategy, Structure and Management Development in the United States and Britain' in K. Kobayashi and H. Morikawa (eds), *Development of Managerial Enterprise* (Tokyo, 1986).

[35] C. H. Lee, 'Regional Growth and Structural Change in Victorian Britain', *Economic History Review*, 2nd Ser., XXXIV (1981).

[36] C. H. Lee, 'The Service Sector, Regional Specialization, and Economic Growth in the Victorian Economy', *Journal of Historical Geography*, 10 (1984).

[37] C. H. Lee, *The British Economy since 1700: A macroeconomic perspective* (1986).

[38] C. H. Lee, 'Growth and Productivity in Services in the Industrial Economies' (forthcoming).

[39] H. Levy, *Monopolies, Cartels and Trusts in British Industry* (1927).

[40] R. Lloyd-Jones and A. A. Le Roux, 'The Size of Firms in the Cotton Industry, 1815–41', *Economic History Review*, 2nd Ser., XXXIII (1980).

[41] R. Lloyd-Jones and A. A. Le Roux, 'Marshall and the Birth and Death of Firms: The Growth and Size Distributions of Firms in the Early Nineteenth Century Cotton Industry', *Business History*, XXIV (1982).

[42] Neil McKendrick and R. B. Outhwaite (eds), *Business Life and Public Policy. Essays in Honour of D. C. Coleman* (Cambridge, 1986).

[43] H. W. Macrosty, *The Trust Movement in British Industry* (1907).

[44] Sheila Mariner, 'English Bankruptcy Records and Statistics before 1850', *Economic History Review*, 2nd Ser., XXXIII(1980).

[45] Alfred Marshall, *Industry and Trade*, 4th edn (1923).

[46] W. H. Marwick, 'The Limited Company in Scottish Economic Development', *Economic History*, III (1937).

[47] Peter Mathias, 'Conflicts of Function in the Rise of Big Business: The British Experience' in H. F. Williamson (ed.), *Evolution of International Business Structures* (Newark, New Jersey, 1975).

[48] M. S. Moss and J. R. Hume, 'Business Failure in Scotland, 1839–1913: A Research Note', *Business History*, XXV (1983).

[49] T. B. Napier, 'The History of Joint Stock and Limited Liability Companies', in *A Century of Law Reform* (1901).

[50] Tony Orhnial (ed.) *Limited Liability and the Corporation* (1982).

[51] P. L. Payne, 'The Emergence of the Large-scale Company in Great Britain', *Economic History Review*, 2nd Ser., XX (1967).

[52] P. L. Payne, *The Early Scottish Limited Companies, 1856–1895* (Edinburgh, 1980).

[53] P. L. Payne, 'Family Business in Britain: An Historical and Analytical Survey' in Akio Okochi and Shigeaki Yasuoka (eds), *Family Business in the Era of Industrial Growth* (Tokyo, 1984).

[54] S. J. Prais, *The Evolution of Giant Firms in Britain* (1976).

[55] S. B. Saul, *The Myth of the Great Depression, 1873–1896*, 2nd edn (1985).

[56] J. Saville, 'Sleeping Partnerships and Limited Liability, 1850–1856', *Economic History Review*, 2nd Ser., VIII (1956).

[57] H. A. Shannon, 'The Coming of General Limited Liability', *Economic History*, II (1931).

[58] H. A. Shannon, 'The First Five Thousand Limited Companies and their Duration', *Economic History*, II (1932).

[59] H. A. Shannon, 'The Limited Companies of 1866 and 1883', *Economic History*, IV (1932–3).

[60] Christine Shaw, 'The Large Manufacturing Employers of 1907', *Business History*, XXV (1983).

[61] John M. Stopford, 'The Origins of British-based Multinational Manufacturing Enterprises', *Business History Review*, XVLIII (1974).

[62] Geoffrey Todd, 'Some Aspects of Joint-stock Companies, 1844–1900', *Economic History Review*, IV (1932–33).

[63] M. A. Utton. 'Some Features of the Early Merger Movements in British Manufacturing Industry', *Business History*, XIV (1972).

[64] E. Welbourne, 'Bankruptcy Before the Era of Victorian Reform', *Cambridge Historical Journal*, IV (1932).

II STUDIES OF PARTICULAR TRADES, INDUSTRIES AND REGIONS

[65] David Alexander, *Retailing in England during the Industrial Revolution* (1970).

[66] G. C. Allen, *The Industrial Development of Birmingham and the Black Country* (1929).

[67] R. C. Allen, 'International Competition in Iron and Steel, 1850–1913', *Journal of Economic History*, XXXIX (1979).

[68] R. C. Allen, 'Entrepreneurship and Technical Progress in the North-east Coast Pig Iron Industry: 1850–1913', *Research in Economic History*, 6 (1981).

[69] P. S. Andrews and E. Brunner, *Capital Development in Steel* (Oxford, 1952).

[70] T. S. Ashton, *Iron and Steel in the Industrial Revolution*, 2nd edn (Manchester, 1951).

[71] T. C. Barker and J. R. Harris, *A Merseyside Town in the Industrial Revolution: St Helens, 1750–1900* (Liverpool, 1954).

[72] J. N. Bartlett, 'The Mechanisation of the Kidderminster Carpet Industry', *Business History*, IX (1967).

[73] J. N. Bartlett, *Carpeting the Millions. The Growth of Britain's Carpet Industry* (Edinburgh, 1978).

[74] Joyce M. Bellamy, 'Cotton Manufacture in Kingston Upon Hull', *Business History*, IV (1982).

[75] Alan Birch, *The Economic History of the British Iron and Steel Industry, 1784–1879* (1967).

[76] D. Bremner, *The Industries of Scotland. Their Rise, Progress and Present Condition* (1869).

[77] D. L. Burn, 'The Genesis of American Engineering Competition', *Economic History*, II (1931).

[78] Duncan Burn, *The Economic History of Steel Making, 1867–1939* (Cambridge, 1961).

[79] T. H. Burnham and G. O. Hoskins, *Iron and Steel in Britain, 1870–1930* (1943).

[80] John Butt, 'The Scottish Cotton Industry during the Industrial Revolution 1780–1840', in *Comparative Aspects of Scottish and Irish Economic and Social History, 1600–1900* (ed. L. M. Cullen and T. C. Smout) (Edinburgh, 1980).

[81] Neil K. Buxton, *The Economic Development of the British Coal Industry* (1978).

[82] I. C. R. Byatt, *The British Electrical Industry, 1875–1914. The Economic Returns of a New Technology* (Oxford, 1979).

[83] R. H. Campbell, *The Rise and Fall of Scottish Industry, 1707–1939* (Edinburgh, 1980).

[84] S. D. Chapman, *The Early Factory Masters* (Newton Abbot, 1967).

[85] S. D. Chapman, 'Fixed Capital Formation in the British Cotton Industry, 1770–1815', *Economic History Review*, 2nd Ser., XXIII (1970).

[86] S. D. Chapman, 'The Cost of Power in the Industrial Revolution: The Case of the Textile Industry', *Midland History*, I (1971).

[87] S. D. Chapman, 'Enterprise and Innovation in the British Hosiery Industry, 1750–1850', *Textile History*, V (1974).

[88] S. D. Chapman, 'Financial Restraints on the Growth of Firms in the Cotton Industry, 1790–1850', *Economic History Review*, XXXII (1979).

[89] S. D. Chapman, 'Working Capital in the British Cotton Industry, 1770–1850', *Mimeo* (undated, *c*.1977).

[90] Sydney J. Chapman, *The Lancashire Cotton Industry. A Study in Economic Development* (Manchester, 1904).

[91] R. A. Church, 'The Effect of the American Export Invasion on the British Boot and Shoe Industry, 1885–1914', *Journal of Economic History*, XXVIII (1968).

[92] R. A. Church, 'Labour Supply and Innovation, 1800–1860. The Boot and Shoe Industry', *Business History* XII (1970).

[93] R. A. Church, 'The British Leather Industry and Foreign Competition 1870–1914', *Economic History Review*, 2nd Ser., XXIV (1971).

[94] R. A. Church, *The History of the British Coal Industry. vol. 3: 1830–1913: Victorian Pre-eminence* (Oxford, 1986).

[95] J. H. Clapham, The Woollen and Worsted Industries (1907).

[96] Archibald and Nan L. Clow, *The Chemical Revolution. A Contribution to Social Technology* (1952).

[97] D. C. Coleman, *The British Paper Industry, 1495–1860* (Oxford, 1958).

[98] W. H. B. Court, *The Rise of Midland Industries, 1600–1838* (1938).

[99] Ian Donnachie, *A History of the Brewing Industry in Scotland* (Edinburgh, 1979).

[100] Baron F. Duckham, *History of the Scottish Coal Industry, vol. I, 1700–1815* (Newton Abbot, 1970).

[101] M. M. Edwards, *The Growth of the British Cotton Trade, 1780–1815* (Manchester, 1867).

[102] Cyril Ehrlich, *The Piano. A History* (1976).

[103] C. Hamilton Ellis, *Nineteenth Century Railway Carriages* (1949).

[104] D. A. Farnie, *The English Cotton Industry and World Markets, 1815–1896* (Oxford, 1979).

[105] Michael Flinn, *The History of the British Coal Industry, vol. 2, 1700–1830: The Industrial Revolution* (1984).

[106] Roderick Floud, *The British Machine and Tool Industry, 1850–1914* (1976).

[107] R. C. Floud, 'The Adolescence of American Engineering Competition, 1860–1900', *Economic History Review*, 2nd Ser., XXVII (1974).

[108] J. H. Fox, 'The Victorian Entrepreneur in Lancashire' in S. P. Bell (ed.), *Victorian Lancashire* (Newton Abbot, 1976).

[109] F. J. Glover, 'The Rise of the Heavy Woollen Trade of the West Riding of Yorkshire in the Nineteenth Century', *Business History*, IV (1961).

[110] L. F. Haber, *The Chemical Industry during the Nineteenth Century* (Oxford, 1958).

[111] Henry Hamilton, *An Economic History of Scotland in the Eighteenth Century* (Oxford, 1963).

[112] A. E. Harrison, 'The Competitiveness of the British Cycle Industry, 1890–1914', *Economic History Review*, 2nd Ser., XXII (1969).

[113] A. E. Harrison, 'Joint-stock Company Flotation in the Cycle, Motor-vehicle and Related Industries, 1882–1914', *Business History*, XXIII (1981).

[114] Elijah Helm, 'The Alleged Decline of the British Cotton Industry', *Economic Journal*, II (1892).

[115] Pat Hudson, *The Genesis of Industrial Capital. A Study of the West Riding wool Textile industry c.1750–1850* (1986).

[116] Charles K. Hyde, *Technological Change and the British Iron Industry 1700–1870* (Princeton, N.J., 1977).

[117] J. B. Jefferys, *Retail Trading in Britain, 1850–1950* (Cambridge, 1954).

[118] D. J. Jenkins and K. G. Ponting, *The British Wool Textile Industry, 1770–1914* (1982).

[119] A. H. John, *The Industrial Development of South Wales* (Cardiff, 1950).

[120] A. H. John and G. Williams (eds), *Glamorgan Country History, vol. V, Industrial Glamorgan from 1700 to 1970* (Cardiff, 1980).

[121] Haydn Jones, *Accounting, Costing and Cost Estimation, Welsh Industry: 1700–1830* (Cardiff, 1985).

[122] S. R. H. Jones, 'Price Associations and Competition in the British Pin Industry, 1814–40', *Economic History Review*, 2nd Ser., XXVI (1973).

[123] William Lazonick, 'Factor costs and the diffusion of ring-spinning in Britain prior to World War I', *Quarterly Journal of Economics*, XCVI (1981).

[124] William Lazonick, 'Production Relations, Labour Productivity and Choice of Technique: British and US Cotton Spinning', *Journal of Economic History*, XLI (1981).

[125] William Lazonick, 'Industrial Organisation and Technical Change: The Decline of the British Cotton Industry', *Business History Review*, LVII (1983).

[126] William Lazonick, 'Rings and Mules in Britain: Reply [to Sandberg, 151]', *Quarterly Journal of Economics*, XCIX (1984).

[127] William Lazonick and William Mass, 'The Performance of the British Cotton Industry, 1870–1913', *Research in Economic History*, 9 (1984).

[128] Bruce Lenman and Kathleen Donaldson, 'Partners' Incomes,

Investment and Diversification in the Scottish Linen Area, 1850–1921', *Business History*, XIII (1971).

[129] Donald M. McCloskey, *Economic Maturity and Entrepreneurial Decline: British Iron and Steel, 1870–1913* (Cambridge, Mass., 1973).

[130] Neil McKendrick, 'The Victorian View of the Midland Potteries', *Midland History*, I (1971).

[131] J. de L. Mann, *The Cloth Industry in the West of Scotland from 1640 to 1880* (Oxford, 1971).

[132] J. D. Marshall, *Furness and the Industrial Revolution* (Barrow, 1958).

[133] R. C. Michie, *Money, Mania and Markets. Investment, Company Formation and the Stock Exchange in Nineteenth-Century Scotland* (Edinburgh, 1981).

[134] W. E. Minchinton, *The British Tinplate Industry: A History* (Oxford, 1957).

[135] Michael S. Moss and John R. Hume, *Workshop of the British Empire. Engineering and Shipbuilding in the West of Scotland* (1977).

[136] A. E. Musson and E. Robinson, 'The Origins of Engineering in Lancashire' *Journal of Economic History*, XX (1960).

[137] T. R. Nevett, *Advertising in Britain. A History* (1982).

[138] G. A. North, *Teeside's Economic Heritage* (Cleveland, 1975).

[139] J. L. Oliver, *The Development and Structure of the Furniture Industry* (1966).

[140] T. G. Orsagh, 'Progress in Iron and Steel: 1870–1913', *Comparative Studies in Society and History*, III (1960–1).

[141] P. L. Payne, *Colvilles and the Scottish Steel Industry* (Oxford, 1979).

[142] D. C. M. Platt, *Latin America and British Trade, 1806–1914* (1973).

[143] Sidney Pollard. 'British and World Shipbuilding, 1890–1914: A Study in Comparative Costs', *Journal of Economic History*, XVII (1957).

[144] Sidney Pollard and Paul Robertson, *The British Shipbuilding Industry, 1870–1914* (Cambridge, Mass., 1979).

[145] Arthur Redford, *Manchester Merchants and Foreign Trade, 1794–1858* (Manchester, 1934).

[146] Arthur Redford, *Manchester Merchants and Foreign Trade, 1850–1939* (Manchester, 1956).

75

[147] A. J. Robertson, 'The Decline of the Scottish Cotton Industry', *Business History*, XII (1970).

[148] D. J. Rowe, *Lead Manufacturing in Britain: A History* (1983).

[149] Lars G. Sandberg, 'American Rings and English Mules: The Role of Economic Rationality', *Quarterly Journal of Economics*, LXXXIII (1969).

[150] Lars G. Sandberg, *Lancashire in Decline. A Study in Entrepreneurship, Technology and International Trade* (Columbus, Ohio, 1974).

[151] Lars G. Sandberg, 'The Remembrance of Things Past: Rings and Mules Revisited', *Quarterly Journal of Economics*, XCIX (1984).

[152] S. B. Saul, 'The American Impact on British Industry, 1895– 1914', *Business History*, III (1960).

[153] S. B. Saul, 'The Motor Industry in Britain' *Business History*, V (1962).

[154] S. B. Saul, 'The Market and Development of the Mechanical Engineering Industries in Britain, 1860–1914', *Economic History Review*, 2nd Ser., XX (1967).

[155] S. B. Saul, Research and Development in British Industry from the end of the Nineteenth Century to the 1960s', in T. C. Smout (ed.), *The Search for Wealth and Stability* (1979).

[156] G. R. Saxonhouse and G. Wright, 'New Evidence on the Stubborn English Mule and the Cotton Industry, 1878– 1920', *Economic History Review*, 2nd Ser., XXXVII (1984).

[157] Seymour Shapiro, *Capital and the Cotton Industry* (Ithaca, New York, 1967).

[158] E. M. Sigsworth, 'The West Riding Wool Textile Industry and the Great Exhibition', *Yorkshire Bulletin of Economic & Social Research*, IV (1952).

[159] Anthony Slaven, *The Development of the West of Scotland* (1975).

[160] Roland Smith, *The Lancashire Cotton Industry and the Great Depression, 1873–1896*, Unpublished Ph.D. thesis, University of Birmingham, 1954.

[161] A. J. Taylor, 'Concentration and Specialisation in the Lancashire Cotton Industry 1825–50', *Economic History Review*, 2nd Ser., I (1949).

[162] W. A. Thomas, *The Provincial Stock Exchange* (1973).

[163] S. Timmins (ed.), *The Resources, Products and Industrial History of Birmingham and the Midland Hardware District* (1866).

[164] Barrie Trinder, *The Industrial Revolution in Shropshire* (1973).

[165] G. Turnbull, *A History of the Calico Printing Industry of Great Britain* (Altrincham, 1951).

[166] R. H. Walters, *The Economic and Business History of the South Wales Steam and Coal Industry, 1840–1914* (New York, 1977).

[167] Kenneth Warren, *Chemical Foundations: The Alkali Industry in Britain to 1926* (Oxford, 1980).

[168] F. A. Wells, *The British Hosiery Trade* (1935).

[169] O. M. Westall (ed.), *The Historian and the Business of Insurance* (Manchester, 1984).

III THE ENTREPRENEUR: DEFINITION, MOTIVATION, RECRUITMENT AND ROLE

[170] H. G. H. Aitken, 'The Future of Entrepreneurial Research', *Explorations in Enrepreneurial History*, 2nd Ser., I (1963).

[171] E. Ames and N. Rosenberg, 'Changing Technological Leadership and Industrial Growth', *Economic Journal*, LXXIII (1963).

[172] T. S. Ashton, *The Industrial Revolution* (1948).

[173] J. W. Atkinson and B. F. Hoselitz, 'Entrepreneurship and Personalilty', *Explorations in Entrepreneurial History*, X (1958).

[174] Reinhard Bendix, *Work and Authority in Industry. Ideologies of Management in the Course of Industrialisation* (New York, 1956).

[175] Reinhard Bendix, 'A Study of Managerial Ideologies', *Economic Development and Cultural Change*, V (1957).

[176] N. M. Bradburn and D. E. Berlew, 'Need for Achievement and English Industrial Growth', *Economic Development and Cultural Change*, X (1961).

[177] Mark Casson, *The Entrepreneur. An Economic Theory* (Oxford, 1982).

[178] S. J. Chapman and F. J. Marquis, 'The Recruiting of the Employing Classes from the Ranks of the Wage-Earners in the Cotton Industry', *Journal of the Royal Statistical Society*, LXXV (1912).

[179] A. H. Cole, 'An Approach to the Study of Entrepreneurship' *Journal of Economic History*, VI Supplement (1946).

[180] François Crouzet (ed.), *Capital Formation in the Industrial Revolution* (1972).

[181] François Crouzet, *The First Industrialists: The Problem of Origins* (Cambridge, 1985).

[182] Charlotte Erickson, *British Industrialists: Steel and Hosiery, 1850–1950* (Cambridge, 1959).

[183] G. H. Evans Jr., 'The Entrepreneur and Economic Theory: A Historical and Analytical Approach', *American Economic Review*, XXXIX (1949).

[184] G. H. Evans Jr, 'Business Entrepreneurs, Their Major Functions and Related Tenets', *Journal of Economic History*, XIX (1959).

[185] D. E. C. Eversley, 'The Home Market and Economic Growth in England, 1750–1780', in *Land, Labour and Population in the Industrial Revolution. Essays Presented to J. D. Chambers* (ed. E. L. Jones and G. Mingay) (1967).

[186] M. W. Flinn, *Origins of the Industrial Revolution* (1966).

[187] M. W. Flinn, 'Social Theory and the Industrial Revolution' in *Social Theory and Economic Change* (ed. T. Burns and S. B. Saul) (1967).

[188] T. R. Gourvish, 'A British Business Elite: the Chief Executive Managers of the Railway Industry, 1850–1923' *Business History Review*, XLVII (1973).

[189] E. E. Hagen, *On the Theory of Social Change* (Homewood, Illinois, 1964).

[190] Leslie Hannah, *Entrepreneurs and the Social Sciences: An Inaugural Lecture* (1983).

[191] R. M. Hartwell, 'Business Management in England during the period of Early Industrialisation: Inducements and Obstacles', in *The Industrial Revolution* (ed. R. M. Hartwell) (Oxford, 1970).

[192] Charles E. Harvey, 'Business History and the Problem of Entrepreneurship: The Case of the Rio Tinto Company, 1873–1939', *Business History*, XXI (1979).

[193] David Hey, *The Rural Metalworkers of the Sheffield Region: A Study of Rural Industry Before the Industrial Revolution* (Leicester, 1972).

[194] Katrina Honeyman, *Origins of Enterprise: Business Leadership in the Industrial Revolution* (Manchester, 1982).

[195] B. F. Hoselitz, 'Entrepreneurship and Capital Formation in France and Britain since 1700', in National Bureau of

Economic Research, *Capital Formation and Economic Growth* (Princeton, 1956).

[196] A. Howe, *The Cotton Masters, 1830–1860* (Oxford, 1984).

[197] Hester Jenkins and D. Caradog Jones, 'Social Class of Cambridge University Alumni of the 18th and 19th Centuries', *British Journal of Sociology*, I (1950).

[198] David J. Jeremy (ed.), *Dictionary of Business Biography*, 5 vols (1984–86).

[199] David J. Jeremy, 'Anatomy of the British Business Elite, 1860–1980', *Business History*, XXVI (1984) (based on the careers of 270 individuals in Volume I of the *DBB*, with surnames beginning with the letters A to C).

[200] Peter Kilby (ed.), *Entrepreneurship and Economic Development* (New York, 1971).

[201] Roy Lewis and Rosemary Stewart, *The Boss, The Life and Times of the British Business Man* (1961).

[202] R. R. Locke, *The End of the Practical Man: Entrepreneurship and Higher Education in Germany, France and Great Britain, 1880–1940* (1984).

[203] D. C. McClelland, *The Achieving Society* (Princeton, New Jersey, 1961).

[204] P. Mantoux, *The Industrial Revolution in the Eighteenth Century* (1923).

[205] Robin Marris, *The Economic Theory of 'Managerial' Capitalism* (1964).

[206] W. M. Mathew, 'The Origins and Occupations of Glasgow Students, 1740–1839', *Past and Present*, No. 33 (April 1966).

[207] Edith Penrose, *The Theory of the Growth of the Firm* (Oxford, 1959).

[208] Harold Perkin, *The Origins of Modern English Society* (1969).

[209] S. Pollard, *The Genesis of Modern Management* (1965).

[210] R. E. Pumphrey, 'The Introduction of Industrialists into the British Peerage: A Study in Adaptation of a Social Institution', *American Historical Review*, LXV (1959).

[211] W. J. Reader, *Professional Men* (1966).

[212] F. Redlich, 'Economic Development, Entrepreneurship and Psychologism: A Social Scientist's Critique of McClelland's *Achieving Society*', *Explorations in Entrepreneurial History*, 2nd Ser., I (1963).

[213] W. D. Rubinstein, 'The Victorian Middle Classes: Wealth, Occupation and Geography', *Economic History Review*, 2nd Ser., XXX (1977).

[214] W. D. Rubinstein, 'Wealth, Elites and Class Structure in Britain', *Past and Present*, No. 76 (1977).

[215] W. D. Rubinstein, *Wealth and the Wealthy in the Modern World* (1980).

[216] W. D. Rubinstein, *Men of Property: The Very Wealthy in Britain since the Industrial Revolution* (1981).

[217] Michael Sanderson, *The Universities and British Industry, 1850–1970* (1972).

[218] Christine Shaw, 'Characteristics of British Business Leaders: Findings from the *Dictionary of Business Biography*' (based on a random sample of 188 cases taken from Volumes 1–4 (A–R) of the DBB [165a]). Paper presented to the Anglo-Japanese Conference on Business History, 1986, *mimeo*.

[219] Anthony Slaven and Sydney Checkland (eds), *Dictionary of Scottish Business Biography, Vol I : The Staple Industries* (Aberdeen, 1986).

[220] Aileen Smiles, *Samuel Smiles and his Surroundings* (1956).

[221] Samuel Smiles, *Self-Help*, Centenary edition (1958).

[222] Jennifer Tann, *The Development of the Factory* (1970).

[223] E. P. Thompson, *The Making of the English Working Class* (1963).

[224] E. P. Thompson, 'Time, Work-Discipline and Industrial Capitalism', *Past and Present*, No. 38 (December 1967).

[225] L. Urwick and E. F. L. Brech, *The Making of Scientific Management* 2 vols (1949).

[226] G. Wilson, *Gentlemen Merchants. The Merchant Community in Leeds, 1700–1830* (Manchester, 1972).

IV THE ENTREPRENEUR: GENERAL ASSESSMENTS OF PERFORMANCE

[227] D. H. Aldcroft, 'The Entrepreneur and the British Economy, 1870–1914', *Economic History Review*, 2nd Ser., XVII (1964).

[228] D. H. Aldcroft, 'Technical Progress and British Enterprise 1875–1914', *Business History*, VIII (1966).

[229] D. H. Aldcroft (ed.), *The Development of British Industry and Foreign Competition, 1875–1914* (1968).

[230] D. H. Aldcroft, 'Investment in and Utilization of Manpower: Great Britain and her rivals, 1870–1914', in Barrie M. Radcliffe (ed.), *Great Britain and Her World, 1750–1914* (Manchester, 1975).

[231] B. W. E. Alford, 'Entrepreneurship, Business Performance and Industrial Development', *Business History*, XIX (1977).

[232] T. J. Byres, *The Scottish Economy During the Great Depression, 1873–1896*, unpublished B.Litt. thesis, University of Glasgow, 1962.

[233] T. J. Byres, 'Entrepreneurship in the Scottish Heavy Industries, 1870–1900', in *Studies in Scottish Business History*; see [362] below.

[234] D. C. Coleman, 'Gentlemen and Players', *Economic History Review*, 2nd Ser., XXVI (1973).

[235] D. C. Coleman and Christine MacLeod, 'Attitudes to New Techniques: British Businessmen, 1800–1950', *Economic History Review*, 2nd Ser., XXXIX (1986).

[236] H. G. Gray and Samuel Turner, *Eclipse or Empire?* (1916).

[237] H. J. Habakkuk, *American and British Technology in the Nineteenth Century* (Cambridge, 1962).

[238] C. K. Harley, 'Skilled Labour and the Choice of Technique in Edwardian Industry', *Explorations in Economic History*, XI (1974).

[239] Ross Hoffman, *Great Britain and the German Trade Rivalry, 1875–1914* (Philadelphia, 1933).

[240] D. S. Landes, 'Entrepreneurship in Advanced Industrial Countries: The Anglo-German Rivalry', in *Entrepreneurship and Economic Growth*. Papers presented at a Conference sponsored jointly by the Committee on Economic Growth of the Social Science Research Foundation and the Harvard University Research Centre in Entrepreneurial History, Cambridge, Massachusetts, 12–13 November 1954.

[241] D. S. Landes, 'Technological Change and Development in Western Europe, 1750–1914', in *The Cambridge Economic History of Europe*, VI. *The Industrial Revolutions and After*, Part I (ed. H. J. Habakkuk and M. Postan) (Cambridge, 1965), subsequently reprinted and extended as *The Unbound Prometheus* (Cambridge, 1969).

[242] D. S. Landes, 'Factor Costs and Demand: Determinants of Economic Growth', *Business History*, VII (1965).

81

[243] A. L. Levine, *Industrial Retardation in Britain, 1880–1914* (1967).

[244] R. R. Locke, 'New Insights from Cost Accounting into British Entrepreneurial Performance, *c*.1914', *The Accounting Historians Journal*, VI (1979).

[245] R. R. Locke, 'Cost Accounting: an Institutional Yardstick for Measuring British Entrepreneurial Performance, *c*.1914', *The Accounting Historians Journal*, VI (1979).

[246] Donald N. McCloskey (ed.), *Essays on a Mature Economy: Britain After 1840. Papers and Proceedings of the M.S.S.B. Conference on the New Economic History of Britain, 1840–1939* (1971).

[247] Donald N. McCloskey and Lars G. Sandberg, 'From Damnation to Redemption: Judgements on the Late Victorian Entrepreneur', *Explorations in Economic History*, IX (1971).

[248] Donald N. McCloskey, 'Did Victorian Britain Fail?', *Economic History Review*, 2nd Ser., XXIII (1970). See the later comment by N. F. R. Crafts and the reply by McCloskey, *Economic History Review*, 2nd Ser., XXXII (1979).

[249] Joel Mokyr, 'Prosperous Interlude', *Economic Development and Cultural Change*, 30 (1982).

[250] Stephen J. Nicholas, 'Total Factor Productivity and the Revision of Post-1870 British Economic Growth', *Economic History Review*, 2nd Ser. XXXV (1982).

[251] Stephen J. Nicholas, 'The Overseas Marketing Performance of British Industry, 1870–1914', *Economic History Review*, 2nd Ser., XXXVII (1984).

[252] Eric M. Sigsworth, 'Some Problems in Business History, 1870–1914', in *Papers of the Sixteenth Business History Conference*, ed. Charles J. Kennedy (Lincoln, Nebraska, 1969).

[253] Martin J. Wiener, *English Culture and the Decline of the Industrial Spirit, 1850–1980* (Cambridge, 1981).

[254] Charles Wilson, 'The Entrepreneur in the Industrial Revolution in Britain', *Explorations in Entrepreneurial History*, III (1955).

[255] Charles Wilson, 'Economy and Society in Late Victorian Britain', *Economic History Review*, 2nd Ser., XVIII (1965).

[256] J. B. Addis, *The Crawshay Dynasty. A Study in Industrial Organisation and Development, 1756–1867* (Cardiff, 1967).

[257] Anon. [various authors] *Fortunes Made in Business*, 3 vols (1884–7).

[258] Anon. *James Finlay and Company Ltd., Manufacturers and East India Merchants, 1750–1950* (Glasgow, 1957).

[259] T. S. Ashton, 'The Records of a Pin Manufacturer, 1814–21', *Economica*, V (1925).

[260] T. S. Ashton, *An Eighteenth Century Industrialist: Peter Stubs of Warrington, 1756–1806* (Manchester, 1939).

[261] T. C. Baxter, *The Glassmakers, Pilkington: 1826–1976* (1977).

[262] J. N. Bartlett, 'Alexander Pirie & Sons of Aberdeen and the Expansion of the British Paper Industry *c*. 1860–1914', *Business History*, XXII (1980).

[263] Rhodes Boyson, *The Ashworth Cotton Enterprise. The Rise and Fall of a Family Firm, 1818–1880* (Oxford, 1970).

[264] Asa Briggs, *Wine for Sale: Victoria Wine and the Liquor Trade, 1860–1984* (1985)

[265] R. H. Campbell, *Carron Company* (Edinburgh and London, 1961).

[266] J. A. Cantell, *James Nasmyth and the Bridgewater Foundry. A study of entrepreneuship in the early engineering industry* (Manchester, 1984).

[267] W. H. Chaloner, 'Robert Owen, Peter Drinkwater and the Early Factory System in Manchester, 1788–1800', *Bulletin of the John Rylands Library*, XXXVII (1954).

[268] Dennis Chapman, 'William Brown of Dundee, 1791–1864: Management in a Scottish Flax Mill, *Explorations in Entrepreneurial History* IV (1952).

[269] S. D. Chapman, 'The Peels in the Early English Cotton Industry', *Business History* XI (1969).

[270] S. D. Chapman, 'James Longsdon (1745–1821), Farmer and Fustian Manufacturer: The Small Firm in the Early English Cotton Industry', *Textile History*, I (1970).

[271] Stanley Chapman, *Jesse Boot of Boots the Chemists* (1974).

[272] S. G. Checkland, *The Mines of Tharsis* (1967).

[273] S. G. Checkland, *The Gladstones. A Family Biography, 1764–1851* (Cambridge, 1971).

[274] R. A. Church, 'An Aspect of Family Enterprise in the Industrial Revolution', *Business History*, IV (1962).

[275] R. A. Church, 'Messrs Gotch & Sons and the Rise of the Kettering Footwear Industry', *Business History*, VII (1966).

[276] R. A. Church, *Kenricks in Hardware. A Family Business, 1791–1966* (Newton Abbot, 1969).

[277] Roy Church, *Herbert Austin and the British Motor Car Industry to 1914* (1979).

[278] D. C. Coleman, *Courtaulds. An Economic and Social History*, 3 vols (1969, 1980).

[279] T. A. B. Corley, *Quaker Enterprise in Biscuits: Huntley and Palmers of Reading, 1822–1972* (1972).

[280] R. P. T. Davenport-Hines, *Dudley Docker, The Life and Times of a Trade Warrior* (Cambridge, 1984).

[281] Ralph Davis, *Twenty-One and a Half Bishop Lane: A History of J. H. Fenner & Co Ltd., 1861–1961* (1961).

[282] I. L. Donnachie and J. Butt, 'The Wilsons of Wilsontown Ironworks (1779–1813): A Study in Entrepreneurial Failure, *Explorations in Entrepreneurial History*, IV (1966–7).

[283] D. A. Farnie, 'John Rylands of Manchester', *Bulletin of the John Rylands University Library of Manchester*, LVI (1973).

[284] R. S. Fitton and A. P. Wadsworth, *The Strutts and the Arkwrights, 1758–1830* (Manchester, 1958).

[285] James Foreman-Peck, 'Diversification and the Growth of the Firm: The Rover Car Company to 1914', *Business History*, XXV (1983).

[286] Edwin Green and Michael Moss, *A Business of National Importance: The Royal Mail Shipping Group, 1902–1937* (1982).

[287] Robert G. Greenhill, 'The Royal Mail Steam Packet Company and the Development of Steamship Links with Latin America, 1875–1900', *Maritime History*, II (1973).

[288] A. E. Harrison, 'F Hopper & Co – The Problems of Capital Supply in the Cycle Manufacturing Industry, 1891–1914', *Business History*, XXIV (1982).

[289] Charles E. Harvey, 'Business History and the Problems of Entrepreneurship: The Case of the Rio Tinto Company, 1873–1939', *Business History*, XXI (1979).

[290] Charles E. Harvey, *The Rio Tinto Company: An Economic History of a Leading International Mining Concern, 1873–1954* (Penzance, 1981).

[291] H. Heaton, 'Benjamin Gott and the Industrial Revolution in Yorkshire', *Economic History Review*, III (1931–2).

[292] John R. Hume and Michael S. Moss, *Beardmore. The History of a Scottish Industrial Giant* (1979).

[293] F. E. Hyde assisted by J. R. Harris, *Blue Funnel: A History of Alfred Holt and Company of Liverpool from 1865 to 1914* (Liverpool, 1956).

[294] F. E. Hyde, *Shipping Enterprise and Management, 1830–1939* (Liverpool, 1967).

[295] R. J. Irving, 'New Industries for Old? Some Investment Decisions of Sir W G Armstrong, Whitworth & Co Ltd., 1900–1914, *Business History*, XVII (1975).

[296] A. H. John (ed.), *The Walker Family, Ironfounders and Lead Manufacturers, 1741–1893* (1951).

[297] A. H. John, *A Liverpool Merchant House: Being the History of Alfred Booth and Company, 1863–1958* (1959).

[298] S. R. H. Jones, 'Hall English & Co., 1913–41. A Study of Entrepreneurial Response in the Gloucester Pin Industry', *Business History*, XVIII (1976).

[299] M. W. Kirby, *Men of Business and Politics. The Rise and Fall of the Quaker Pease Dynasty of North-east England, 1700–1943* (1984).

[300] C. H. Lee, *A Cotton Enterprise, 1795–1840. A History of M'Connel and Kennedy, Fine Cotton Spinners* (Manchester, 1972).

[301] John C. Logan, 'The Dumbarton Glass Works Company: A Study in Entrepreneurship', *Business History*, XIV (1972).

[302] Neil McKendrick, 'Josiah Wedgwood: An Eighteenth-Century Entrepreneur in Salesmanship and Marketing Techniques', *Economic History Review*, 2nd Ser., XII (1960).

[303] Neil McKendrick, 'Josiah Wedgwood and Factory Discipline', *Historical Journal*, IV (1961).

[304] Neil McKendrick, 'Josiah Wedgwood and the Factory System', *Proceedings of the Wedgwood Society*, No. 5 (1963).

[305] Neil McKendrick, 'Josiah Wedgwood and Thomas Bentley: An Inventor-Entrepreneur Partnership in the Industrial Revolution', *Transactions of the Royal Historical Society*, XIV (1964).

[306] Neil McKendrick, 'Josiah Wedgwood and Cost Accounting in the Industrial Revolution', *Economic History Review*, 2nd Ser., XXIII (1970).

[307] M. H. MacKenzie, 'Cressbrook and Litton Mills, 1779–1835', *Derbyshire Archaeological Journal*, LXXXVIII (1968).

[308] Sheila Marriner, *Rathbones of Liverpool, 1845–74* (Liverpool, 1961).

[309] Sheila Marriner and Francis E. Hyde, *The Senior: John Samuel Swire: 1825–98* (Liverpool, 1967).

[310] John J. Mason, 'A Manufacturing and Bleaching Enterprise during the Industrial Revolution: The Sykeses of Edgeley, *Business History*, XXIII (1981).

[311] Peter Mathias, *Retailing Revolution: A History of Multiple Retailing in the Food Trades based upon the Allied Supplies Group of Companies* (1967).

[312] Jocelyn Morton, *Three Generations in a Family Textile Firm* (1971).

[313] Michael S. Moss, 'William Todd Lithgow – Founder of a Fortune', *Scottish Historical Review*, LXII (1983).

[314] A. E. Musson, 'An Early Engineering Firm: Peel, William & Co. of Manchester', *Business History*, III (1960).

[315] A. E. Musson, *Enterprise in Soap and Chemicals, Joseph Crosfield & Sons Ltd., 1815–1965* (Manchester, 1965).

[316] A. E. Musson, 'Joseph Whitworth and the Growth of Mass-Production Engineering', *Business History*, XVII (1975).

[317] Robert Owen, *The Life of Robert Owen, written by Himself*, (1857).

[318] P. L. Payne, *Rubber and Railways in the Nineteenth Century* (Liverpool, 1961).

[319] S. Piggott, *Hollins: A Study of Industry, 1784–1949*, (Nottingham, 1949).

[320] A. Raistrick, *Dynasty of Iron Founders* (Newton Abbot, 1970).

[321] W. J. Reader, *Imperial Chemical Industries, A History*, vol. I, *The Forerunners, 1870–1926* (1970).

[322] W. J. Reader, *A House in the City: A Study of the City and the Stock Exchange based on the records of Forster and Braithwaite, 1825–1975* (1985).

[323] Goronwy Rees, *St Michael: A History of Marks and Spencer* (1969).

[324] Sir Wemyss Reid, *Memoirs and Correspondence of Lyon Playfair* (1900).

[325] H. W. Richardson and J. M. Bass, 'The Profitability of Consett Iron Company Before 1914', *Business History*, VII (1965).

[326] W. G. Rimmer, *Marshalls of Leeds, Flax Spinners, 1788–1886* (Cambridge, 1960)

[327] A. J. Robertson, 'Robert Owen, Cotton Spinner: New Lanark, 1800–1825' in *Robert Owen, Prophet of the Poor*, ed. S. Pollard and J. Salt (1971).

[328] Eric Robinson, 'Boulton & Fothergill, 1762–1782, and the Birmingham Export of Hardware', *University of Birmingham Historical Journal*, VII (1959).

[329] Eric Robinson, 'Eighteenth Century Commerce and Fashion: Matthew Boulton's Marketing Techniques', *Economic History Review*, 2nd Ser., XVI (1963).

[330] E. Roll, *An Early Experiment in Industrial Organisation, Being a History of Boulton and Watt, 1775–1805* (1930).

[331] Mary Rose, 'The Role of the Family in providing Capital and Managerial Talent in Samuel Greg & Co., 1784–1840', *Business History*, XIX (1977).

[332] Mary Rose, 'Diversification of Investment by the Greg Family, 1800–1914', *Business History*, XXI (1979).

[333] Mary B. Rose, *The Gregs of Quarry Bank Mill. The rise and decline of a family firm, 1750–1914* (Cambridge, 1986).

[334] J. D. Scott, *Vickers. A History* (1962).

[335] Eric M. Sigsworth, *Black Dyke Mills* (Liverpool, 1958).

[336] A. Slaven, 'A Glasgow Firm in the Indian Market: John Lean & Sons, Muslin Weavers', *Business History Review*, XLIII (1969).

[337] Roland Smith, 'An Oldham Limited Liability Company, 1875–1896' *Business History*, IV (1961).

[338] G. B. Sutton, 'The Marketing of Ready Made Footwear in the Nineteenth Century. A Study of the Firm of C. & J. Clark', *Business History*, VI (1964).

[339] G. B. Sutton, *A History of Shoemaking in Street, Somerset: C. & J. Clark, 1833–1903* (1979).

[340] Clive Trebilcock, *The Vickers Brothers: Armaments and Enterprise, 1854–1914* (1977).

[341] Clive Trebilcock, *Phoenix Assurance and the Development of British Insurance, vol. I: 1782–1870* (Cambridge, 1986).

[342] R. E. Tyson, *The Sun Mill Company Limited: A Study in Democratic Investment, 1858–1959*, unpublished M. A. Thesis, University of Manchester, 1962.

[343] R. E. Tyson, 'William Marcroft (1822–94) and the Limited Liability Movement in Oldham', *Transactions of the Lancashire and Cheshire Antiquarian Society*, 80 (1980).

[344] David Wainwright, *Broadwood by Appointment* (1982).

[345] R. A. Wells, *Hollins and Viyella. A Study in Business History* (Newton Abbot, 1968).

[346] Charles Wilson, *The History of Unilever*, 2 vols (1954).

[347] Charles Wilson, *First with the News: A History of W. H. Smith, 1792–1972* (1985).

[348] Charles Wilson and William Reader, *Men and Machines. A History of D. Napier & Sons, Engineers Ltd., 1808–1858* (1958).

VI GUIDES TO BUSINESS ARCHIVES AND BUSINESS HISTORIES

[349] David Allen, 'Surveys of Records in the British Isles', *Aslib Proceedings* (1971).

[350] T. C. Barker, R. H. Campbell, P. Mathias and B. S. Yamey, *Business History*, Rev. edn (1971).

[351] Joyce M. Bellamy (ed.), *Yorkshire Business Histories: A Bibliography* (Bradford, 1970).

[352] H. A. L. Cockerill and Edwin Green, *The British Insurance Business, 1547–1970* (1976).

[353] B. R. Crick and M. Alman, *A Guide to Manuscripts Relating to America in Great Britain and Ireland* (1961).

[354] Charles Harvey, 'Business Records at the Public Record Office', *Business Archives*, No. 52 (November, 1986).

[355] S. Horrocks, *Lancashire Business Histories* (Manchester, 1971).

[356] Patricia Hudson, *The West Riding Wool Textile Industry: A Catalogue of Business Records* (Edlington, Wiltshire, 1975).

[357] Joan Lane, *Register of Business Records of Coventry and Related Areas* (Coventry, 1977).

[358] Jane Low, *A Guide to Sources in the History of the Cycle and Motor Industries in Coventry, 1880–1939* (Coventry, 1982).

[359] Sheila Marriner, 'Company Financial Statements as Source Material for Business Historians', *Business History*, XXII (1980).

[360] P. Mathias and A. W. H. Pearsall (eds), *Shipping: A Survey of Historical Records* (Newton Abbott, 1971).

[361] E. R. J. Owen and Frank Dux, *A List of the Location of Records belonging to British Firms and to British Businessmen active in the Middle East, 1800–1950* (Oxford: Middle East Centre, 1973).

[362] P. L. Payne (ed.), *Studies in Scottish Business History* (1967).

[363] L. S. Pressnell and J. Orbell (eds), *A Guide to the Historical Records of British Banking* (Aldershot, 1985).

[364] T. Rath, 'Business Records in the Public Record Office in the Age of the Industrial Revolution', *Business History*, XVII (1975).

[365] Lesley Richmond and Bridget Stockford, *Company Archives. The Survey of the Records of 1000 of the First Registered Companies in England and Wales* (Aldershot, 1986).

[366] L. A. Ritchie, *Modern British Shipbuilding. A Guide to Historical Records* (Maritime Monographs and Reports, No.48, 1980).

[367] R. A. Storey (ed.), *Sources of Business History in the National Register of Archives: First Five-year Cumulation* (Historical Manuscripts Commission, 1971).

[368] Peter Walne (ed.), *A Guide to Manuscript Sources for the History of Latin America and the Caribbean in the British Isles* (1973).

An annual list of new accessions of business records in county record offices and other repositories reporting to the National Register of Archives is published in *Business Archives, The Journal of the Business Archives Council,* which also carries a useful list of business histories. In 1984, it was announced in *Business History*, XXVI (1984), 80, that, as a preliminary to the preparation of a published guide to manuscript sources for the history of business and industry in the nineteenth and early twentieth centuries, the Royal Commission on Historical Manuscripts had constructed an index of all relevant information that it possessed about the records of individual companies. The index is available for public consultation and use in the Commission's search room. Those particularly concerned with Scottish business should consult the Newsletter of the Business Archives Council of Scotland, an occasional publication superseded in 1976 by *Scottish Industrial History*. Useful information on archives and sources and ongoing research is contained in the *Business History Newsletter* produced by the Business History Unit of the University of London.

Index

copper industry 16

corporate economy, emergence
of 17, 20, 27

cotton industry 15, 16, 18, 22,
24, 25, 26, 30, 31, 32, 33, 35–6,
37, 45, 47–8, 56, 62

Courtaulds 36, 66

Cowling, K., Stoneman, P., *et al.*
66

Crafts, N. F. R. 30

Crawshay & Co. 32, 37

Crouzet, François 21–2, 48

cutlery industry 18

cycle industry 46

Dale, David 15

Darwin, John 37

Davenport-Hines, R. P. T. 56

Davis, Ralph 65

Davis, R. B. 65

debentures 17

d'Eichthal, G. 62

Dictionary of Business Biography
25, 28, 56, 59

*Dictionary of Scottish Business
Biography* 25, 59

diversification 18

Docker, Dudley 56

DuBois, A. B. 16

Dugdale, John 36

Dundonald, Lord 33

Eaton, Richard 38

educational system 26, 50, 55

Elbaum, Bernard 54, 66

engineering industry 18, 25, 26,
32–3, 45, 46, 48–9

English Sewing Cotton Ltd 19

entrepreneurs: function of 11–
13, 15, 53, 54; independence
of 53, 65; motivation of 23,
59; origins of 21–2, 25–7;
religious persuasion of 22;
reputation of 9–10, 29–30, 58

entrepreneurship: definition of
11–13; dynamic nature of 12,
13, 35; methods of measuring
quality of 37, 39, 45, 46–7,

48–9, 54, 64; quality of
British 9, 10, 13, 29–57

Erickson, Charlotte 22, 26, 59

Evans, G. H. 11

family businesses 13, 15, 16, 18,
22, 25, 39, 40, 42–3

Farnie, D. A. 62

Fenner, J. H. & Co. 65

Finlay, James and Kirkham 15

firm, the, structure of 12, 14–
20; age structure of 24–5,
34–5

flax-spinners 24, 32, 35

Flinn, M. W. 12, 22

Floud, R. 45, 48

footwear industry 25, 46, 52

fraudulent practices 31

Garbett, Samuel 33

Gatrell, V. A. C. 15, 62

Girouard, Mark 62

Gott, Benjamin 30, 32

Gourvish, T. R. 27

Gray, Herbert and Turner,
Samuel 55, 64

Great Exhibition, 1851 40

Green, Edwin and Moss,
Michael 56

Greenwood & Batley 48, 53

Greg, Edward Hyde 61

Guests of Dowlais 37

Habakkuk, H. J. 44

Hagan, E. E. 22

Harley, C. K. 55

Harmsworth, Alfred 45

Harris, Frank 62

Harrison, A. E. 46

Harvey, Charles E. 54

Hay, Donald A. and Morris,
Derek J. 66

Hobsbawm, E. J. 43, 49, 51, 53

Hodge, P. R. 38

Hoffman, R. J. S. 64, 65

Holdsworth, W. B. & Co. 35